BBQ

food for friends

BBQ
food for friends

Jane Lawson and Vanessa Broadfoot

whitecap

Contents

Getting started
Making the most of your BBQ

Cooking food over a fire has a very long history. No-one is sure when our early ancestors first discovered the taste benefits of exposing their food to heat, but as successful experiments go, it's a hard one to top. Ever since, we have been baking, boiling, smoking, frying and, because it would be silly to abandon such a good idea, barbecuing.

Cooking outdoors has come a long way from those early bonfires. This collection of recipes takes you from an easy, mid-week dinner, right through to a Sunday afternoon alfresco feast with friends. You'll find that there's no limit to what can be cooked on a barbecue, from full roasts to seafood and even your favourite desserts.

Barbecues may be a homemade construction consisting of a grill plate balanced over a wood fire, or a state-of-the-art giant with every possible optional extra. Regardless of what yours looks like, you'll find recipes in here that not only challenge your idea of what barbecuing is all about, but also fix it in your mind as one of the most fun and delicious ways to prepare food.

Methods of cooking

Indirect and direct are the main cooking methods when you are using a barbecue. Make sure you set up your barbecue properly to shorten cooking times and ensure perfectly cooked meals.

For direct cooking

KETTLE BARBECUE, start the barbecue and let the briquettes burn for about 45 minutes before you begin cooking. For a medium–hot barbecue, use about 60, for a lower temperature, about 45 briquettes should be enough. If you need to lower the temperature when the fire is already set, just spritz the coals with a light spray of water, but if you want to increase the heat, you will need to add more briquettes and wait for the heat to develop.
GAS OR ELECTRIC BARBECUE, light the barbecue and let it heat for 10 minutes before cooking.

For indirect cooking

KETTLE BARBECUE, start the barbecue (putting the fuel on each side to leave room for the drip tray) and leave the fire to develop for about 45 minutes. Put a drip tray between the coals and sit the top grill in place. Position the food so that it is over the drip tray and cover it with the lid. Keep the bottom vents open so that the heat circulates evenly, and don't open the lid unless it's really necessary — the more often the heat is allowed to escape, the longer your cooking time will be.
GAS OR ELECTRIC BARBECUE, it's best to check the manufacturers' instructions on how to set up your barbecue for indirect cooking. Generally, the outside burners are set to medium–low and the food sits in the middle of the barbecue. This means that the heat can circulate around the meat without burning it underneath.

Types of BBQ

There are two main methods of cooking on a barbecue. The first is to cook food over direct heat, for example over a wood fire or barbecue fuel briquettes located directly under a grill or plate. The food must be turned during cooking so that it cooks evenly on both sides.

The other method is to use indirect heat, for which you will need a barbecue with some kind of hood or cover. This method of cooking works a bit like an oven, by circulating the heat around the food, and it is mainly used for roasting larger cuts of meat, giving them a distinctive barbecue flavour.

WOOD-BURNING FIXED BARBECUES are the traditional, backyard barbecue — usually a fairly simple construction in the form of an elevated grill plate with a fire burning underneath. Although easy to use and available to anyone with some clear space, a few bricks and a grill, the basic design lends itself only to fairly simple methods of cooking. Heat regulation is usually achieved by adjusting the fire and waiting for it to reach the right temperature, although it's more desirable to let the flames die down and cook over a pile of glowing embers which give off a more constant heat.

KETTLE BARBECUES are portable, come in a range of sizes and are designed for both direct and indirect cooking. A kettle barbecue has a rounded base which holds barbecue fuel briquettes on a metal grill. If you want to cook with direct heat, simply grill the food over the coals. If you want to cook using the indirect method, arrange the briquettes in two piles on opposite sides of the bottom grill and put a drip-tray between them before inserting the top grill. To give the heat a boost, open the vents in the outer shell of the barbecue — this will allow air to circulate, making the briquettes burn faster and hotter. To keep the temperature a little cooler, leave the vents closed.

GAS BARBECUES are available in a huge variety of sizes and shapes, from small portables to huge, wagon-style barbecues that come with a hood, rotisserie and workbench on the side. They are convenient and simple to operate, usually requiring only 10 minutes or so to heat up, and the turn of a knob to regulate temperature. Some work by means of a flame under the barbecue plate, while others use the flame to heat a bed of reusable volcanic rock. If your barbecue has a lid or hood, you can also cook using indirect heat.

ELECTRIC BARBECUES operate on a principle similar to that of gas barbecues, by heating the grill plate on which the food is cooked. They can be less convenient than a gas barbecue as they require access to an electricity outlet and the heat produced may not be as even or as strong as that produced by a gas or solid-fuel barbecue.

BBQ tips

- Food cooked on a grill plate can also be cooked on an open grill provided it is large enough not to fall through the holes.

- Food cooked on an open grill may also be cooked on a grill plate.

- Invest in a small fire extinguisher, in case of emergency.

- Bring the meat to room temperature before cooking it, but don't leave it sitting at room temperature for more than 20 minutes.

- Always soak wooden skewers for an hour before use to prevent them from charring on the grill.

- Always make sure that the barbecue is clean before lighting it. If possible, clean it out as soon as it is cool enough, brushing or scraping the grill plates and discarding ash and embers.

- Assemble all the equipment you will need before you start cooking so that you won't have to leave the food unattended.

- Make sure that the barbecue is in a sheltered position and on a level surface, away from wooden fences, overhanging trees or anything else that may be flammable.

- Brush or spray the barbecue with oil before lighting it in case the oil comes in contact with the flame and flares up. To stop food from sticking, brush it with oil just before cooking it, make sure the grill plate is the correct temperature and don't turn the food until the surface of the food has cooked and 'released' itself naturally from the grill.

- If you wish to use the marinade to baste, you must boil it, then let it simmer for at least 5 minutes before basting so that any bacteria from the raw meat are not transferred to the cooked meat.

- If you are basting the food with a sugary glaze, apply it only in the last 10 minutes of cooking, as it will tend to burn on the grill.

- Salt meat just before barbecuing as salt will quickly draw moisture out of the meat if it is left.

The perfect steak

Everybody has a preference for how they like their steak cooked and there are many variables to consider. The cut of meat, the thickness of the steak, how hot the barbecue is and the distance of the plate from the heat source are all factors contributing to how the meat will cook. These timings are approximate for a 3 cm (1¼ inch) thick steak cooked over medium–high heat.

- For rare cook the steak for 2 minutes on each side. The steak should feel quite soft when pressed lightly with tongs and will be very red and moist inside.
- For medium rare cook the steak for about 3 minutes on each side. The steak will still feel quite soft when gently pressed, but the internal colour will be a lighter red with pink juices.
- For medium cook the steak for 4 minutes on each side or until juice comes to the surface, then turn it over and cook until juice appears on the other side. The meat will feel slightly springy to the touch and the inside will be pink in the middle and brown near the edges, with clear pink juices.
- For well done cook the steak for 5 minutes on each side. Sear it until juice is pooling on top, then turn and cook until the juice is pooling again. At this stage reduce the heat slightly so that the steak can continue to cook through without burning. The steak should be quite firm when pressed, with clear juices and no sign of pink inside. A well done steak will tend to be rather dry, no matter what cut of meat is used.

Food never tastes better than when it is cooked outdoors. Whether you use traditional wood, or modern briquettes or gas, you'll still get that sought-after, flame-grilled flavour. Nearly every culture in the world has a tradition of gathering for a meal cooked in this way. It's a ritual that transforms ordinary food into a delicious feast, delicately smoked or bursting with robust flavours and juices. Venture beyond the confines of the kitchen, bring your barbecue out of weekday exile and get it going with fantastic everyday dinners, or celebrate a big event with surprisingly little effort. We've drawn on every corner of the world to bring you meals from Asia, North Africa, Europe, the Americas and Australia, so you can follow the recipes as they stand or pick and mix a Moroccan roast, an Italian salad and finish with an Asian-inspired dessert. Best of all, gather your friends and family around for one of the most important of occasions — sharing good food and good company.

main meals

STEAK SANDWICH WITH BALSAMIC ONIONS AND SUN-DRIED TOMATO AND BASIL CREAM

125 g (1/2 cup) sour cream

40 g (1 1/2 oz) sun-dried tomatoes, well
  drained and finely chopped

3 garlic cloves, crushed

2 tablespoons finely chopped basil leaves

2 teaspoons lemon juice

2 red onions

2 tablespoons olive oil

2 tablespoons balsamic vinegar

1 tablespoon brown sugar

8 large slices of sourdough bread

400 g (14 oz) piece of fillet steak, cut into
  1 cm (1/2 inch) thick slices

55 g (4 handfuls) baby rocket (arugula)
  leaves, rinsed and well drained

SUITABLE FOR ANY BARBECUE
COOKING TIME: 15 MINUTES
SERVES 4

1 Preheat the barbecue to medium–high direct heat. Mix the sour cream, sun-dried tomatoes, garlic, basil and lemon juice in a small bowl and season the mixture to taste.

2 Thinly slice the onions, separate the rings and toss them with 1 tablespoon of the olive oil. Spread the onion across the flat grill plate and cook it for 10 minutes, or until it is softened and starting to brown, then gather the rings into a pile and pour the combined balsamic vinegar and sugar over them. Turn the onion so that it is well coated in the balsamic mixture, then spread it out a little and cook for a few more minutes, or until it is slightly glazed. Remove the onion from the barbecue and toast the bread on the chargrill plate for 30 seconds on each side, or until grill marks appear.

3 Brush the steaks with a little olive oil and season them with salt and freshly ground black pepper. Chargrill them for 1 minute on each side for medium–rare, or 2 minutes for well done.

4 To make each sandwich, put a piece of steak on a slice of toasted bread and top with the onion, a dollop of the sour cream mixture and some rocket leaves. Finish with a second piece of toast and serve immediately. Better yet, put out all of the different elements and let everyone make their own sandwich.

MARINATED LAMB WITH MOROCCAN SPICED CARROT SALAD

LAMB MARINADE

15 g (1/2 cup) finely chopped flat-leaf (Italian)
    parsley

20 g (1/3 cup) finely chopped coriander
    (cilantro) leaves

4 garlic cloves, crushed

1 tablespoon paprika

1 teaspoon dried thyme

125 ml (1/2 cup) olive oil

60 ml (1/4 cup) lemon juice

2 teaspoons ground cumin

4 x 250 g (9 oz) lamb rumps or pieces
    of tenderloin, trimmed

CARROT SALAD

4 carrots, peeled, trimmed and halved
    on the diagonal

80 ml (1/3 cup) olive oil

2 teaspoons ground cumin

95 g (1/2 cup) Kalamata olives, pitted
    and halved lengthways

5 g (1/4 cup) flat-leaf (Italian) parsley

1 teaspoon harissa

2 tablespoons extra virgin olive oil

1 tablespoon red wine vinegar

SUITABLE FOR A FLAT OR RIDGED
    GRILL PLATE
COOKING TIME: 40 MINUTES
SERVES 4

1 Mix the parsley, coriander, garlic, paprika, thyme, oil, lemon juice and 1 1/2 teaspoons cumin together in a non-metallic dish. Score diagonal lines in the fat on the lamb pieces with a sharp knife, then put them in the marinade, turning so they are evenly coated. Cover and refrigerate for at least 2 hours or overnight.

2 To make the spiced carrot salad, preheat the flat plate to low. Bring a saucepan of salted water to the boil and blanch the carrots for 3 minutes, or until they just begin to soften. Drain, pat dry with paper towels, then toss them with 2 tablespoons of the olive oil and 1 teaspoon of the cumin. Cook the carrots for 25 minutes, turning them once so they are cooked through and golden all over.

3 While the carrots are still warm, cut them into thin diagonal slices and toss them with the olives and parsley. Mix the harissa with 1 tablespoon of water, add the extra virgin olive oil, red wine vinegar, remaining olive oil and remaining cumin, and whisk it together. Pour the dressing over the salad and season to taste with salt and pepper.

4 Increase the heat under the flat plate to medium direct heat. Season the lamb with white pepper, the remaining 1/2 teaspoon of cumin and some salt. Cook the rumps fat side up for 3 minutes and then cook the other side for 2–3 minutes, making sure the fat is well cooked. Take the lamb off the barbecue as soon as it is done, cover it with foil and put it aside to rest for about 5 minutes before carving. Serve it with the warm carrot salad.

LEMON AND THYME ROASTED CHICKEN WITH ZUCCHINI

1 x 1.8 kg (4 lb) chicken

12 garlic cloves, unpeeled

10 sprigs lemon thyme

1 lemon, halved

1 tablespoon olive oil

8 small zucchini (courgettes), halved
  lengthways

2 tablespoons chopped flat-leaf (Italian)
  parsley

1 tablespoon plain (all-purpose) flour

250 ml (1 cup) chicken stock

SUITABLE FOR A COVERED BARBECUE

COOKING TIME: 1 HOUR 5 MINUTES

SERVES 4

1 Remove the giblets and any large fat deposits from inside the chicken, then pat it dry inside and out with paper towels. Season the cavity with salt and pepper and stuff it with the unpeeled garlic cloves and the sprigs of thyme. Rub the skin with the cut lemon, making sure that it is evenly coated all over, then brush it with 2 teaspoons of the oil and season with salt and black pepper.

2 Preheat a kettle or covered barbecue to medium indirect heat, with a drip tray underneath the grill. Position the chicken on the barbecue directly over the drip tray, close the hood and roast the chicken for 1 hour, or until the juices run clear when it is pierced with a skewer between the thigh and the body.

3 When the chicken has been cooking for about 40 minutes, toss the zucchini with the remaining olive oil and season it with salt and black pepper. Arrange the zucchini on the grill around the chicken, re-cover the kettle and cook the chicken and the zucchini for 20–25 minutes, or until the zucchini is tender, but not soggy. Put the zucchini in a serving dish and sprinkle it with the parsley. When the chicken is ready, remove it from the barbecue, cover it loosely with foil and leave it to rest for 10 minutes. Remove the garlic from the chicken cavity but do not peel the cloves.

4 If you would like gravy to go with the chicken, pour the contents of the drip tray into a container and skim off as much fat as possible. Tip the remaining juices into a saucepan, add the flour and stir well to combine. Cook the gravy over medium heat for 3–4 minutes, or until it has thickened, then add the chicken stock and any juices that have been released from the chicken while it was resting. Bring the gravy to the boil, then reduce the heat and simmer it for 3–4 minutes. Season the gravy to taste, strain it into a jug and serve it with the chicken, garlic and zucchini.

SWORDFISH WITH TOMATO BUTTER AND GRILLED ASPARAGUS

100 g (3½ oz) butter, softened

50 g (⅓ cup) semi-dried (sun-blushed)
   tomatoes, finely chopped

2 tablespoons baby capers in brine, drained
   and crushed

1½ tablespoons shredded basil leaves

4 garlic cloves, crushed

60 ml (¼ cup) extra virgin olive oil

300 g (10½ oz) slender asparagus spears,
   trimmed

4 swordfish steaks

SUITABLE FOR ANY BARBECUE
COOKING TIME: 10 MINUTES
SERVES 4

1 Put the butter in a bowl with the tomato, capers, basil and two cloves of crushed garlic, and mash it all together. Shape the flavoured butter into a log, then wrap it in baking paper and twist the ends to close them off. Refrigerate the butter until it is firm, then cut it into 1 cm (½ inch) slices and leave it, covered, at room temperature until you are ready to use it.

2 Mix 2 tablespoons of the oil and the remaining garlic in a small bowl. Toss the asparagus spears with the oil until they are well coated, season them with salt and pepper, and leave for 30 minutes.

3 Preheat the ridged grill plate to high direct heat. Brush the swordfish steaks with the remaining oil and cook them for 2–3 minutes on each side or until they are just cooked through. Don't overcook the fish as residual heat will continue to cook the meat after it has been removed from the barbecue. Put a piece of the tomato butter on top of each steak as soon as it comes off the barbecue and season to taste. Cook the asparagus on the chargrill plate, turning it regularly, for 2–3 minutes, or until it is just tender. Serve the asparagus immediately with the fish.

BRUSCHETTA WITH MUSHROOMS AND MUSTARD CREME FRAICHE

5 small field mushrooms (about 300 g/
    10½ oz), quartered
1 red onion, halved and thinly sliced
170 ml (⅔ cup) olive oil
3 garlic cloves, crushed
1½ tablespoons chopped oregano leaves
60 g (¼ cup) crème fraîche
1 teaspoon Dijon mustard
1 loaf ciabatta bread
60 ml (¼ cup) olive oil, extra
1 large garlic clove, extra, peeled
    and halved
small oregano leaves
150 g (6 handfuls) mixed lettuce leaves
2 tablespoons extra virgin olive oil
1 tablespoon lemon juice

SUITABLE FOR A FLAT OR RIDGED
    GRILL PLATE
COOKING TIME: 10 MINUTES
SERVES 6

1 Put the mushrooms and onion in separate bowls and season each with salt and pepper. Whisk together the oil, crushed garlic and oregano and pour two-thirds of the mixture over the mushrooms and the rest over the onion. Toss the vegetables so that they are well coated in the marinade, then cover and refrigerate both of the bowls for 30 minutes. Mix the crème fraîche and mustard together, then refrigerate it until you are ready to use it.

2 Heat the barbecue to medium direct heat. Cut the bread into twelve 1 cm (½ inch) thick slices and brush both sides of each slice with the extra oil. Toast the bread on the chargrill plate for 1–2 minutes on each side or until it is golden and lightly charred, then rub one side of each slice with the cut side of the garlic clove. Cook the onion on the flat plate, tossing it gently, for 2–3 minutes or until soft and golden. Next, cook the mushrooms on the flat plate for 2 minutes on each side or until they are cooked through, then toss the onion and mushrooms together.

3 Arrange the mushrooms and onion on the garlic-rubbed side of the bread slices and top with a teaspoon of the mustard crème fraîche. Garnish each piece with oregano leaves and season with salt and pepper. Toss the mixed lettuce leaves with the extra virgin olive oil and lemon juice, and serve with the bruschetta.

BOURBON-GLAZED BEEF RIBS WITH SWEET POTATO

MARINADE

1/4 teaspoon chilli powder

1/2 teaspoon chilli flakes

1/2 teaspoon celery salt

1/8 teaspoon cayenne pepper

500 ml (2 cups) cider vinegar

60 ml (1/4 cup) lemon juice

6 garlic cloves, crushed

1 tablespoon paprika

1 teaspoon garlic powder

1 teaspoon onion powder

125 ml (1/2 cup) Worcestershire sauce

3 kg (6 lb 8 oz) beef loin ribs (see Notes)

SWEET POTATOES

60 g (2 1/4 oz) butter, at room temperature

1 tablespoon maple syrup

1 tablespoon chopped pecan nuts

1/2 teaspoon garlic salt

4 x 200 g (7 oz) sweet potatoes

BARBECUE SAUCE

500 ml (2 cups) tomato sauce

55 g (1/4 cup) soft brown sugar

80 ml (1/3 cup) bourbon

60 g (1/4 cup) Dijon mustard

1 tablespoon Tabasco sauce

2 teaspoons paprika

1 teaspoon garlic powder

1 teaspoon onion powder

1 1/2 tablespoons Worcestershire sauce

SUITABLE FOR A COVERED BARBECUE

COOKING TIME: 3 HOURS 15 MINUTES

SERVES 4–6

1 Mix together the marinade ingredients with 1/4 teaspoon pepper and 1/4 teaspoon salt, and rub the marinade all over the ribs. Put the ribs in a non-metallic bowl, cover them and refrigerate overnight.

2 Mash together the butter, maple syrup, pecans, garlic salt and some black pepper, and cover until you are ready to dish up. Put all of the barbecue sauce ingredients in a saucepan and stir them together. Simmer the sauce over low heat for 15 minutes, or until the mixture has thickened, stirring constantly. Be careful while stirring the sauce as it might splatter a bit.

3 Preheat a kettle or covered barbecue to very low indirect heat. Remove the ribs from the marinade and baste them all over with the barbecue sauce. Cook them on the flat plate for 3 hours, or until they are very tender, turning and basting them every 30 minutes.

4 Arrange the whole sweet potatoes on a lightly greased baking tray and add them to the barbecue 45 minutes before the ribs have finished cooking.

5 Remove the ribs and sweet potatoes from the barbecue, slice each sweet potato down the middle and top each with some of the flavoured butter. Cut between the ribs to separate them and serve the ribs with the sweet potatoes.

❋ Notes: Beef loin ribs are also known as beef shortribs. Make sure the barbecue temperature remains low and constant. If the heat is too high, the ribs will burn before they become tender.

LAMB KOFTA WITH BABA GANOUJ, TABBOULEH AND GRILLED OLIVES

LAMB KOFTA WITH BABA GANOUJ AND GRILLED OLIVES

KOFTA

1 red onion, finely chopped

25 g (3/4 cup) chopped flat-leaf (Italian)
    parsley

25 g (1/2 cup) chopped coriander (cilantro)
    leaves

15 g (1/4 cup) chopped mint leaves

1 tablespoon paprika

1 tablespoon ground cumin

1 1/2 teaspoons allspice

1/2 teaspoon ground ginger

1/2 teaspoon chilli flakes

1.2 kg (2 lb 11 oz) minced (ground) lamb

60 ml (1/4 cup) soda water

BABA GANOUJ

2 (820 g/1 lb 12 oz) eggplants (aubergines)

2 garlic cloves, finely chopped

1/4 teaspoon ground cumin

60 ml (1/4 cup) lemon juice

2–2 1/2 tablespoons tahini

60 ml (1/4 cup) olive oil

1 tablespoon chopped flat-leaf (Italian)
    parsley

1/2 teaspoon sumac

200 g (7 oz) Kalamata olives

olive oil, for brushing

4 pieces pitta bread

SUITABLE FOR A COVERED BARBECUE
COOKING TIME: 35 MINUTES
SERVES 4

1 To make the kofta, put the onion, herbs and spices in a food processor and blend until they are combined. Season the mixture with 2 teaspoons salt and some freshly ground black pepper, then add the minced lamb to the food processor and get the motor going again. Add the soda water in a thin stream until the mixture forms a smooth paste, then cover and refrigerate for at least 2 hours, or overnight.

2 To make the baba ganouj, preheat a covered barbecue chargrill plate to medium–high. Prick the eggplants a few times with a fork and cook them, covered, for 20 minutes, or until they are soft and wrinkled, turning them halfway through the cooking time. Put the eggplants in a colander and leave them for 30 minutes to allow any bitter juices to drain, then peel and discard the skin and roughly chop the flesh. Put the eggplant in a food processor with the garlic, cumin, lemon juice, tahini and olive oil and process the baba ganouj for 30 seconds, or until it is smooth and creamy. Season to taste with salt, then cover and refrigerate it. Sprinkle the baba ganouj with the parsley and sumac before serving.

3 Soak four wooden skewers in cold water for 1 hour. Divide the lamb mixture into 12 portions and mould each portion into a torpedo shape, using damp hands to stop the meat from sticking to you, then cover and refrigerate the kofta. Thread the olives onto the soaked skewers.

4 When you're ready to cook the kofta, preheat the flat grill plate to medium–high direct heat. Brush the kofta lightly with olive oil and cook them, turning frequently, for 10–12 minutes, or until they are evenly browned and cooked through. When the kofta are nearly cooked, add the olives to the barbecue for 1–2 minutes. Serve the kofta immediately with pitta bread, the baba ganouj, grilled olives and some tabbouleh.

TABBOULEH

130 g (³/4 cup) burghul (bulgar)

3 ripe tomatoes

1 telegraph (long) cucumber

80 ml (¹/3 cup) lemon juice

60 ml (¹/4 cup) olive oil

1 tablespoon extra virgin olive oil

4 spring onions (scallions), sliced

120 g (4 cups) chopped flat-leaf
   (Italian) parsley

10 g (¹/4 oz) chopped mint

Cover the burghul with 500 ml (2 cups) water and leave it for 1¹/2 hours. Cut the tomatoes in half, squeeze the halves gently to remove any excess seeds and cut the flesh into 5 mm (¹/4 inch) cubes. Cut the cucumber in half lengthways, remove the seeds and cut the flesh into 5 mm (¹/4 inch) cubes. Drain the burghul, squeezing out any excess water, and spread it out across a clean tea towel for 30 minutes to dry. Whisk together the lemon juice and 1¹/2 teaspoons of salt until they are well combined. Season the dressing with pepper, then slowly whisk in the olive oil and extra virgin olive oil. Put the burghul in a large bowl and add the tomato, cucumber, spring onion, parsley and mint. Toss the dressing with the tabbouleh, then cover and refrigerate.

29

PORTUGUESE SPATCHCOCK

1 red onion, chopped
6 garlic cloves, chopped
3 teaspoons grated lemon zest
2 teaspoons chilli flakes
1 1/2 teaspoons paprika
60 ml (1/4 cup) oil
60 ml (1/4 cup) red wine vinegar
4 x 500 g (1 lb 2 oz) spatchcocks (poussin)
10 g (1/3 cup) chopped flat-leaf (Italian)
   parsley
lemon halves

SUITABLE FOR ANY BARBECUE
COOKING TIME: 20 MINUTES
SERVES 4

1 Put the onion, garlic, lemon zest, chilli flakes, paprika, oil and vinegar in a food processor and blend them to a smooth paste.

2 Cut each of the spatchcocks down the backbone with sharp kitchen scissors and press down on the breastbone to flatten it out. Score the flesh and brush it with the spice mixture, then put the spatchcocks in a non-metallic dish, cover and refrigerate overnight.

3 Preheat the chargrill plate to low–medium direct heat. Grill the spatchcocks for 10 minutes on each side, or until they are cooked through (test by piercing the thigh with a skewer — if the juices run clear, they are ready), then sprinkle them with parsley and serve with the lemon halves.

Note: Try grilling the lemon halves for a bit of extra flavour.

STUFFED PORK CHOPS WITH CHARGRILLED SPRING ONIONS

2 tablespoons dry sherry

4 dried dessert figs

1 tablespoon butter

60 ml (1/4 cup) olive oil

1 small onion, finely diced

2 garlic cloves, crushed

1 large Granny Smith apple, peeled, cored
   and grated

2 tablespoons slivered almonds, lightly
   toasted

1 tablespoon finely chopped sage leaves

6 large pork loin chops (250 g/9 oz each)
   on the bone

16 large bulb spring onions (scallions),
   green parts removed, halved

SUITABLE FOR A FLAT OR RIDGED
   GRILL PLATE
COOKING TIME: 30 MINUTES
SERVES 6

1 Bring the sherry and 1 tablespoon of water to the boil in a small saucepan. Soak the figs in the hot sherry mixture for 20 minutes, then slice them finely and keep the soaking liquid to use later.

2 Heat the butter and 1 tablespoon of olive oil in a frying pan, add the onion and garlic, and cook over low heat for 5 minutes or until they are softened. Add the grated apple, figs and sherry liquid, and simmer for a further 5 minutes, or until the apple has softened and most of the liquid has evaporated. Remove the pan from the heat and stir in the almonds and sage, then season well and allow the mixture to cool.

3 Trim the pork chops of any excess fat and make an incision into the middle of the chop from the side. Be careful — you only want to make a pocket in the flesh and not cut right through. Fill the pocket with the apple and fig stuffing, pushing it well into the cavity so that none is spilling out; you should fit about 1 1/2 tablespoons of filling in each chop. Brush the chops all over with 1 tablespoon of the olive oil, and season with salt and freshly ground black pepper. Toss the spring onion with the remaining oil, and season it well.

4 Heat the chargrill plate to medium direct heat. Cook the chops for 8 minutes on each side, or until the outside is slightly charred and the meat is cooked through. While the chops are cooking, add the spring onions to the chargrill plate and cook them for 10 minutes, or until they are softened. Serve the chops and spring onions as soon as they come off the barbecue. .

MISO-GLAZED SALMON AND EGGPLANT SALAD WITH SESAME DRESSING

5 tablespoons sesame seeds, lightly toasted

70 g (1/4 cup) white miso

1 tablespoon sake

1 tablespoon mirin

1 tablespoon sugar

60 ml (1/4 cup) dashi stock

1 large eggplant (aubergine), cut into 1 cm
 (1/2 inch) rounds

2 garlic cloves, crushed

60 ml (1/4 cup) olive oil

2 teaspoons dark soy sauce

60 ml (1/4 cup) dashi stock, extra

1 teaspoon sugar, extra

1 teaspoon grated fresh ginger

150 g (5 1/2 oz) snow pea shoots

400 g (14 oz) daikon, julienned

4 salmon fillets, skin removed

SUITABLE FOR ANY BARBECUE
COOKING TIME: 10 MINUTES
SERVES 4

1 To make the miso glaze, put the sesame seeds in a spice grinder or mortar and pestle and grind them until they have a rough, flaky texture. Whisk the miso, sake, mirin, sugar and dashi stock together until smooth and stir in half of the crushed sesame seeds.

2 Put the eggplant rounds in a large bowl with the combined garlic and oil, season them with salt and pepper and toss until the rounds are well coated.

3 To make the dressing, whisk together the soy sauce, extra dashi and sugar, ginger and remaining crushed sesame seeds. Put the snow pea shoots and daikon in a large bowl, add the soy dressing and toss them until they are well combined. Cover the bowl and refrigerate until needed.

4 Heat the barbecue to medium–high direct heat. Cook the eggplant on the chargrill plate for 3–4 minutes on each side, or until it has softened, then allow it to cool slightly and cut it into quarters. Brush both sides of each salmon fillet with the miso glaze and cook them on the flat plate for 2 minutes each side, or until they are almost cooked through, brushing with the glaze while they are cooking. Flake the fillets with a fork and toss them through the salad with the eggplant. Season and serve the salad straight away.

ROAST BEEF WITH BARBECUE SAUCE

2 tablespoons paprika

1 tablespoon onion powder

1 tablespoon garlic powder

2 teaspoons sugar

1 teaspoon chilli powder

60 ml (1/4 cup) oil

1 x 1.5 kg (3 lb 5 oz) piece beef fillet

BARBECUE SAUCE

2 tablespoons oil

1 small onion, finely chopped

4 garlic cloves, crushed

1/2 teaspoon chilli flakes

1 tablespoon paprika

1/2 teaspoon smoked paprika

375 ml (1 1/2 cups) tomato sauce

125 ml (1/2 cup) beer

60 ml (1/4 cup) cider vinegar

80 ml (1/3 cup) brown sugar

2 tablespoons Dijon mustard

80 ml (1/3 cup) Worcestershire sauce

SUITABLE FOR A COVERED BARBECUE
COOKING TIME: 1 HOUR 25 MINUTES
SERVES 6

1 Mix the paprika, onion powder, garlic powder, sugar, chilli powder, 2 teaspoons ground black pepper, 2 teaspoons salt and the oil in a small bowl. Rub the mixture all over the beef fillet, then cover it with plastic wrap and refrigerate overnight.

2 To make the barbecue sauce, put the oil in a small saucepan over medium heat, add the onion, garlic and chilli flakes, and cook them for 5 minutes or until the onion is soft. Add the remaining ingredients and 60 ml (1/4 cup) water, and let the sauce simmer over low heat for 20 minutes, or until it is slightly thickened. Season well and let it cool.

3 Preheat a kettle or covered barbecue to medium indirect heat. Put the beef fillet in the middle of the barbecue and cook, covered, for 40 minutes for rare beef. If you would like medium beef, leave it to roast for another 10 minutes.

4 Brush the barbecue sauce all over the beef fillet and cook it, covered, for another 10 minutes. Remove the beef from the barbecue, cover it loosely with foil and let it rest for 10 minutes before carving and serving it with the remaining barbecue sauce.

CHICKEN TIKKA WITH GARLIC NAAN AND APPLE RAITA

100 g (1/3 cup) tikka paste

60 g (1/4 cup) thick yoghurt

600 g (1 lb 5 oz) chicken breast fillet, cut
  into 3 cm (1 1/4 inch) cubes

2 small red onions, quartered

oil, for brushing

2 tablespoons chopped coriander (cilantro)
  leaves

APPLE RAITA

1 green apple, grated

2 teaspoons lemon juice

60 g (1/4 cup) sour cream

3 tablespoons chopped mint leaves

GARLIC NAAN

1 garlic clove, crushed

2 tablespoons butter, softened

4 plain naan bread

SUITABLE FOR ANY BARBECUE

COOKING TIME: 15 MINUTES

SERVES 4

1 Stir the tikka paste and yoghurt, together, add the chicken and turn it until it is evenly coated in the tikka mixture. Cover the chicken with plastic wrap and refrigerate it for 4 hours or overnight.

2 To make the raita, put the grated apple, lemon juice, sour cream and mint in a small bowl and stir it all together. Cover the bowl and refrigerate it until you are ready to dish up. Mash the crushed garlic and butter together and brush one side of each piece of naan with about 2 teaspoons of garlic butter.

3 Soak four wooden skewers in cold water for 1 hour and preheat the barbecue to low–medium direct heat. Thread the chicken and onion pieces onto the skewers and cook them on the flat plate for 5–6 minutes on each side, turning once. A little before the chicken is ready, lightly brush the chargrill plate with some oil. Grill the naan, buttered side down, for 1–2 minutes, or until the bread is golden and marked. Turn it and grill for another minute on the other side.

4 Sprinkle the skewers with the chopped coriander and serve them with the garlic naan and apple raita.

CHARGRILLED CAULIFLOWER SALAD WITH TAHINI DRESSING AND GREMOLATA

TAHINI DRESSING

65 g (¼ cup) tahini

1 garlic clove, crushed

60 ml (¼ cup) rice vinegar

1 tablespoon oil

¼ teaspoon sesame oil

1 teaspoon lemon juice

2 teaspoons sesame seeds, toasted

1 tablespoon finely chopped flat-leaf (Italian)
   parsley

½ small garlic clove, finely chopped

½ teaspoon finely grated lemon zest

1 cauliflower (about 1.8 kg/4 lb)

2 tablespoons oil

2 baby Cos (romaine) lettuces, washed and
   drained

50 g (1¾ oz) watercress leaves, washed
   and drained

SUITABLE FOR A FLAT OR RIDGED
   GRILL PLATE
COOKING TIME: 10 MINUTES
SERVES 4

1 To make the dressing, whisk the tahini, garlic, rice vinegar, oils, lemon juice and 1 tablespoon of water together and season it to taste. Stir the sesame seeds, parsley, garlic and lemon zest together.

2 Divide the cauliflower into large florets and cut each floret into 1 cm (½ inch) thick slices, then brush the slices with oil and season them well. Preheat the chargrill plate to medium direct heat and chargrill the cauliflower pieces for 6–8 minutes, or until they are cooked and golden on both sides.

3 Arrange the Cos leaves and watercress on a serving dish and top them with the chargrilled cauliflower slices. Drizzle the tahini dressing over the cauliflower, sprinkle it with the sesame seed mixture and serve it while it is still piping hot.

ROAST LAMB WITH RATATOUILLE

1 x 2.5 kg (5 lb 8 oz) leg of lamb
6 garlic cloves, peeled
2 tablespoons rosemary leaves
1 tablespoon olive oil

RATATOUILLE
1 bulb of garlic
80 ml (1/3 cup) olive oil
6 Roma (plum) tomatoes, halved lengthways
4 baby eggplants (aubergines), cut into
   1 cm (1/2 inch) pieces on the diagonal
3 zucchini (courgettes), cut into 1 cm
   (1/2 inch) pieces on the diagonal
2 red capsicums (peppers), seeded and cut
   into wedges
2 red onions, cut into 1 cm (1/2 inch) thick
   rounds
2 tablespoons balsamic vinegar

SUITABLE FOR A COVERED BARBECUE
COOKING TIME: 1 HOUR 30 MINUTES
SERVES 6

1 Make 12 small incisions in the fleshy parts of the lamb. Cut the garlic cloves in half lengthways, and push them into the incisions with the rosemary leaves. Rub the lamb with the oil and season it liberally with salt and pepper. Preheat a kettle or covered barbecue to medium indirect heat, put the lamb in the middle of the barbecue, replace the lid, and let it roast for 1 hour 30 minutes.

2 Meanwhile, to make the ratatouille, trim the top of the garlic bulb so that the cloves are just exposed, drizzle 1 teaspoon of olive oil over the cut end and wrap the bulb in foil. Put the garlic in the barbecue with the lamb for 30 minutes, or until it has softened. Brush the vegetables with 2 tablespoons of olive oil and add them to the barbecue when the garlic has been cooking for about 15 minutes. Cook the vegetables for 5–8 minutes on each side, or until they are marked and cooked through, then put them in a large bowl. Squeeze the garlic cloves out of their skins and add them to the vegetables. Mix the balsamic vinegar and remaining olive oil together, gently toss it with the ratatouille and season well.

3 When the lamb is ready, remove it from the barbecue and let it rest, covered, for 10 minutes before carving and serving it with the ratatouille and any juices that have been released while it rested.

CHINESE BARBECUE PORK WITH PANCAKES

2 tablespoons sugar

2 tablespoons light soy sauce

2 tablespoons hoisin sauce

2 tablespoons dark soy sauce

2 tablespoons rice wine

2 tablespoons yellow bean paste
  (see Notes)

2 teaspoons sesame oil

1 teaspoon five-spice powder

2 garlic cloves, crushed

1 teaspoon finely grated fresh ginger

1 kg (2 lb 4 oz) pork fillet

1 tablespoon honey

24 Peking duck pancakes (see Notes)

1 cucumber, seeded and cut into 8 cm x
  5 mm (3 x 1/4 inch) strips

4 spring onions (scallions) cut into 8 cm x
  5 mm (3 x 1/4 inch) strips

125 ml (1/2 cup) plum sauce

SUITABLE FOR ANY BARBECUE

COOKING TIME: 25 MINUTES

SERVES 6

1 Put the sugar, light soy sauce, hoisin sauce, dark soy sauce, rice wine, yellow bean paste, sesame oil, five-spice powder, garlic, ginger and 1/4 teaspoon ground white pepper in a large, non-metallic bowl. Mix them together well, add the pork and turn it until it is thoroughly coated in the marinade, then cover and refrigerate it for at least 2 hours, or overnight.

2 Take the pork out of the refrigerator and let it come back to room temperature. Drain the marinade into a small saucepan, add the honey and simmer it over low heat for 5 minutes, or until it has reduced slightly. Preheat the chargrill plate to medium direct heat and cook the pork on the chargrill plate for 20 minutes, or until it is caramelized and cooked through, turning and basting it with the honey marinade mixture in the last 5–8 minutes of cooking. Allow the fillet to rest for 5 minutes before slicing.

3 Wrap the pancakes in foil and sit them on a warm place on the grill while the pork is resting so that they heat through without cooking or burning. Put the sliced pork and warm pancakes out with the rest of the fillings and let everyone make up their own pancake parcels by wrapping some sliced pork, cucumber, spring onion and plum sauce in a pancake.

✳ Notes: Yellow bean paste is made from fermented yellow soy beans and is available from Asian grocery stores.
Peking duck pancakes are available frozen from Asian grocery stores or from Chinese barbecue meat shops.

TUNA BURGER WITH HERBED MAYONNAISE

4 garlic cloves, crushed

2 egg yolks

250 ml (1 cup) light olive oil

3 tablespoons chopped flat-leaf (Italian)
   parsley

1 tablespoon chopped dill

2 teaspoons Dijon mustard

1 tablespoon lemon juice

1 tablespoon red wine vinegar

1 tablespoon baby capers in brine, drained

4 anchovy fillets in oil, drained

4 x 150 g (5½ oz) tuna steaks

2 tablespoons olive oil

2 red onions, thinly sliced

4 large round bread rolls, halved and
   buttered

100 g (3½ oz) mixed lettuce leaves

SUITABLE FOR A FLAT OR RIDGED
   GRILL PLATE
COOKING TIME: 10 MINUTES
SERVES 4

1 Put the garlic and egg yolks in the bowl of a food processor and process them together for 10 seconds. With the motor running, add the oil in a very thin, slow stream and when the mixture starts to thicken start adding the oil a little faster. Keep going until all of the oil has been added and the mixture is thick and creamy, then add the parsley, dill, mustard, lemon juice, vinegar, capers and anchovies, and process until the mixture is smooth. Refrigerate the mayonnaise until you need it.

2 Preheat the chargrill plate to high direct heat. Brush the tuna steaks with 1 tablespoon of olive oil and cook them for 2 minutes on each side, or until they are almost cooked through. Add the remaining olive oil to the onion, toss to separate and coat the rings, and cook on the flat plate for 2 minutes, or until the onion is soft and caramelized. Toast the rolls, buttered side down, on the chargrill plate for 1 minute, or until they are marked and golden.

3 Put some lettuce, a tuna steak, some of the onion and a dollop of herbed mayonnaise on one half of each roll. Season with salt and pepper, top with the other half of the roll and serve immediately.

✳ Note: Any left-over herbed mayonnaise will keep for about 1 week in an airtight container in the refrigerator. Try tossing it through thickly sliced, steamed potatoes for a delicious snack or side dish.

BEEF AND MOZZARELLA BURGERS WITH CHARGRILLED TOMATOES

500 g (1 lb 2 oz) minced (ground) beef

160 g (2 cups) fresh breadcrumbs

1 small red onion, very finely chopped

4 garlic cloves, crushed

30 g (1/2 cup) finely shredded basil leaves

50 g (1 3/4 oz) pitted black olives, finely
   chopped

1 tablespoon balsamic vinegar

1 egg

8 pieces mozzarella 2 cm x 3 cm x 5 mm
   (3/4 x 1 1/4 x 1/4 inch)

olive oil spray

CHARGRILLED TOMATOES

6 Roma (plum) tomatoes

1 1/2 tablespoons olive oil

SUITABLE FOR A FLAT OR RIDGED
   GRILL PLATE

COOKING TIME: 20 MINUTES

SERVES 4

1 Put the beef, breadcrumbs, onion, garlic, basil, olives, balsamic vinegar and egg in a large bowl and season well with salt and pepper. Use your hands to mix it all together, then cover and refrigerate the mixture for 2 hours.

2 Divide the beef mixture into eight portions and roll each portion into a ball. Push a piece of mozzarella into the middle of each ball, then push the mince mixture over to cover the hole and flatten the ball to form a patty.

3 To make the chargrilled tomatoes, slice the tomatoes in half lengthways and toss them with the olive oil. Spray the flat plate with olive oil and preheat it to high direct heat. Cook the tomatoes, cut side down, for 8 minutes then turn them over and cook for another 5 minutes or until they are soft.

4 Cook the patties on one side for 5 minutes then flip them and cook for another 5 minutes or until they are completely cooked through and the cheese has melted. Serve the rissoles and chargrilled tomatoes with a fresh green salad.

MARINATED LAMB CUTLETS WITH ORANGE SWEET POTATOES AND GINGER NORI BUTTER

16 lamb cutlets

125 ml (1/2 cup) Japanese plum wine
  (see Note)

2 tablespoons Japanese soy sauce

1 teaspoon finely grated fresh ginger

2 garlic cloves, crushed

few drops sesame oil

4 x 200 g (7 oz) orange sweet potatoes

oil, for brushing

GINGER NORI BUTTER

90 g (3 1/4 oz) butter, softened

1 1/2 tablespoons very finely shredded nori

2 teaspoons finely grated fresh ginger

SUITABLE FOR A COVERED BARBECUE
COOKING TIME: 1 HOUR
SERVES 4

1 Trim the lamb cutlets of any excess fat. Mix together the plum wine, soy sauce, grated ginger, garlic and sesame oil, add the cutlets to the marinade and turn them a few times so they are well coated. Cover the dish with plastic wrap and refrigerate it for 3 hours. To make the ginger nori butter, mash the butter, shredded nori and grated ginger together and season with pepper.

2 Preheat a covered barbecue to medium indirect heat. Brush the potatoes with a little oil and wrap them in a double layer of foil, put them on the barbecue and replace the lid. Roast the potatoes for 50 minutes, or until they are tender when pierced with a sharp knife, then remove them from the heat and leave the barbecue uncovered.

3 Drain the marinade into a small saucepan and boil it over high heat for 5 minutes or until it is reduced by about half. Brush the chargrill plate with a little oil and cook the cutlets for 1 minute, then turn them over, brush with the reduced marinade and cook them for another minute. This will give a rare cutlet, so if you like your meat cooked a little more, you'll need to extend the cooking time on each side by a minute or so. Remove the cutlets from the barbecue, brush them with the remaining reduced marinade, cover, and leave them to rest for 3 minutes. Serve the lamb with the orange sweet potatoes topped with nori butter. They are delicious with an Asian leaf salad (try a few handfuls each of mizuna, baby tatsoi and Chinese cabbage) or steamed Asian greens.

❋ Note: Japanese plum wine is available from specialist Japanese grocery stores and some liquor suppliers.

CHICKEN CAESAR SALAD

CAESAR DRESSING

1 egg yolk

1 garlic clove, crushed

3 anchovy fillets

1 teaspoon Dijon mustard

125 ml (1/2 cup) oil

1 tablespoon lemon juice

1/2 teaspoon Worcestershire sauce

15 g (1/2 oz) grated Parmesan cheese

4 chicken thigh fillets, trimmed of fat
   and sinew

80 ml (1/3 cup) olive oil

12 x 1 cm (1/2 inch) thick slices baguette

1 garlic clove, halved

4 rashers bacon

2 baby Cos (romaine) lettuces, well washed
   and drained

extra anchovies, optional

SUITABLE FOR ANY BARBECUE
COOKING TIME: 20 MINUTES
SERVES 4–6

1   Put the egg yolk, garlic, anchovy fillets and Dijon mustard in a food processor and blend them together. With the motor running, gradually add the oil in a thin stream and process until the mixture becomes thick. Stir in the lemon juice, Worcestershire sauce and Parmesan, and season with salt and pepper to taste. Put the chicken thighs in a bowl with 1 tablespoon of olive oil, season them well with salt and pepper and turn them so they are coated in the oil.

2   Preheat the chargrill plate to medium–high direct heat. Brush the baguette slices with the remaining olive oil, and toast them on the chargrill plate for 1 minute on each side, or until they are crisp and marked. Rub both sides of each piece of toast with the cut clove of garlic and keep them warm.

3   Grill the chicken thighs on the chargrill plate for 5 minutes on each side, or until they are cooked through. Leave the thighs to rest for 1 minute then cut them into 1 cm (1/2 inch) strips. Cook the bacon for 3 minutes on each side or until it is crispy, then break it into 2 cm (3/4 inch) pieces.

4   Tear the Cos leaves into bite-sized pieces and toss them in a large bowl with the dressing, bacon and chicken. Serve with the garlic croutons and let people add extra anchovies to taste.

SPICE RUBBED PORK KEBABS WITH GARLIC SAUCE AND FENNEL SALAD

SPICE-RUBBED PORK KEBABS WITH GARLIC SAUCE

800 g (1 lb 12 oz) pork neck fillet, trimmed
2 teaspoons fennel seeds
2 teaspoons coriander seeds
1 tablespoon olive oil

GARLIC SAUCE
4 garlic cloves, coarsely chopped
1 thick slice of white bread, crusts removed
60 ml (1/4 cup) olive oil
1 1/2 tablespoons lemon juice
lemon wedges
pitta bread

SUITABLE FOR ANY BARBECUE
COOKING TIME: 10 MINUTES
SERVES 4

1 Soak 8 wooden skewers in cold water for 1 hour and cut the pork into 2 cm (3/4 inch) cubes. Dry-fry the fennel and coriander seeds for about 30 seconds, or until they are fragrant, then grind them in a spice grinder or mortar and pestle. Mix the ground spices with the olive oil and toss the pork in it until the meat is well coated. Cover the dish and refrigerate it for 2 hours.

2 To make the garlic sauce, crush the garlic cloves in a mortar and pestle with 1/2 teaspoon salt until you have a very smooth paste. Tear the bread into pieces and leave it in a bowl with enough warm water to cover it. Let it soak for 5 minutes then squeeze out the bread and add it to the garlic, a little at a time, pounding as you go until you have a smooth paste. Keep pounding as you add the olive oil, 1 tablespoon at a time until it has all been added, then add 3 tablespoons of boiling water, one tablespoon at a time, and stir in the lemon juice. You should end up with a smooth, thick paste.

3 Thread the pork onto the soaked skewers and season the kebabs well with salt and pepper. Preheat the chargrill plate to medium–high direct heat and grill the kebabs for 10 minutes, or until they are cooked through, turning them halfway through the cooking time. Drizzle the kebabs with a little garlic sauce and put the rest of the sauce in a small bowl to serve at the table. Serve with the fennel salad, lemon wedges and warm pitta bread.

Note: You can also use a small food processor to make the garlic sauce. Beware! It has a very strong flavour, only a little is required.

FENNEL SALAD

2 large fennel bulbs
1 tablespoon lemon juice
1 tablespoon extra virgin olive oil
2 teaspoons red wine vinegar
150 g (5½ oz) Niçoise olives, pitted

Trim the fennel bulbs, reserving the fronds, and discard the tough outer layers. Using a very sharp knife, slice the fennel lengthways as thinly as possible and put it in a bowl of very cold water with the lemon juice. Just before you are ready to serve, drain the fennel well, pat it dry with paper towels and toss it in a bowl with the olive oil and red wine vinegar. Finely chop the fronds, add them to the fennel with the olives and season to taste with freshly ground black pepper.

SPICY CRAB WITH SINGAPORE-STYLE PEPPER SAUCE

2 kg (4 lb 8 oz) blue crabs

150 g (5½ oz) butter

2 tablespoons finely chopped garlic

1 tablespoon finely chopped fresh ginger

1 small red chilli, seeded and finely chopped

3 tablespoons ground black pepper

2 tablespoons dark soy sauce

2 tablespoons oyster sauce

1 tablespoon palm sugar or soft brown sugar

1 spring onion (scallion), green part only, sliced thinly on the diagonal

SUITABLE FOR ANY BARBECUE
COOKING TIME: 20 MINUTES
SERVES 4–6

1 To prepare the crabs pull back the apron and remove the top shell from each crab (it should come off easily and in one piece). Remove the intestine and the grey feathery gills, then use a large sharp knife to cut the crab in half lengthways, leaving the legs attached. Crack the thick part of the legs with the back of a heavy knife or crab crackers to allow the flavours to seep in and to make it easier to extract the meat.

2 Heat the barbecue flat plate or chargrill plate to medium–high direct heat. Cook the crab pieces on the barbecue for 5–8 minutes on each side, or until they have turned orange and are cooked through. Heat a wok over medium heat (you'll need to do this on the stovetop if you don't have a special wok burner on your barbecue), and stir-fry the butter, garlic, ginger, chilli and pepper together for 30 seconds or until they are fragrant. Add the combined soy and oyster sauces and sugar to the wok, and simmer the sauce for another minute or until it becomes glossy.

3 Toss the cooked crab in the sauce until it is completely coated, then arrange it on a serving dish, sprinkle with the spring onion and serve with steamed rice and a green salad. This dish is very rich and very messy to eat — make sure there are plenty of paper towels or napkins on hand to clear up spills.

LEMON AND SAGE MARINATED VEAL CHOPS WITH ROCKET

4 veal chops

2 tablespoons olive oil

1 tablespoon lemon juice

4 strips lemon zest

10 g (¼ cup) roughly chopped sage leaves

3 garlic cloves, peeled and bruised

lemon wedges

ROCKET SALAD

100 g (4 handfuls) rocket (arugula), washed
  and picked

1 avocado, sliced

1½ tablespoons extra virgin olive oil

2 teaspoons balsamic vinegar

SUITABLE FOR ANY BARBECUE
COOKING TIME: 15 MINUTES
SERVES 4

1 Trim any fat and sinew from the chops and put them in a shallow, non-metallic dish with the olive oil, lemon juice, lemon zest, sage and garlic. Turn the chops so that they are evenly coated, then season them with freshly ground black pepper, cover and refrigerate for 4 hours or overnight.

2 Put the rocket in a large serving bowl and scatter the avocado over it. Drizzle the olive oil and balsamic vinegar over the salad, season it with a little salt and black pepper and toss gently.

3 Preheat the chargrill plate to medium–high direct heat. Remove the chops from the marinade, season with salt and chargrill them for 5–6 minutes on each side, or until they are cooked to your liking. Remove the chops from the barbecue, cover them loosely with foil and let them rest for 5 minutes.

4 Put the chops on a serving dish, drizzle them with any juices that have been released while they rested and serve with the rocket salad and lemon wedges.

SPICED DUCK BREAST WITH PEACH AND CHILLI SALAD

6 ripe peaches

1 lime plus 1 tablespoon lime juice, extra

1 tablespoon extra virgin olive oil

1 small red chilli, seeded and finely sliced

2 tablespoons chopped mint leaves

4 duck breasts

2 teaspoons ground coriander

lime wedges

SUITABLE FOR A FLAT OR RIDGED
 GRILL PLATE

COOKING TIME: 10 MINUTES

SERVES 4

1 Dip the peaches into a saucepan of boiling water for 5 seconds then plunge them into iced water. Remove the skins, which should slip off easily. Cut each peach in half, remove the stone, then cut each half into eight wedges. Peel the lime, removing all the pith, and separate the lime sections by carefully cutting each piece away from the membrane. Toss the peach slices with the lime segments, extra lime juice, olive oil, chilli and mint, and season with a little pepper.

2 Trim the duck breasts of fat and sinew, and sprinkle each breast with the ground coriander.

3 Preheat the flat plate to medium direct heat and cook the duck on the flat plate for 4 minutes or until the skin is golden, then turn it and cook for another 4 minutes. Turn the breasts over again and cook them for 1 minute longer to make the skin crispy, then leave to rest in a warm place for 10 minutes.

4 Slice each breast into four pieces on the diagonal and serve them with the peach salad and lime wedges.

MOROCCAN PUMPKIN ON PISTACHIO COUSCOUS

250 ml (1 cup) vegetable stock

185 g (1 cup) instant couscous

1 tablespoon butter

2 garlic cloves, crushed

1 small onion, finely diced

2 tablespoons finely chopped flat-leaf
(Italian) parsley

2 tablespoons finely chopped coriander
(cilantro) leaves

35 g (^{1}/$_4$ cup) roasted, shelled and roughly
chopped pistachio nuts

2 tablespoons ras el hanout or Moroccan
spice blend (see Note)

250 g (1 cup) plain Greek-style yoghurt

1 tablespoon lemon juice

1 tablespoon honey

1 kg (2 lb 4 oz) pumpkin

2 tablespoons olive oil

SUITABLE FOR A COVERED BARBECUE
COOKING TIME: 50 MINUTES
SERVES 4–6

1 Bring the vegetable stock to the boil, pour it over the couscous and stir to combine them. Cover the bowl with plastic wrap and leave it for 10 minutes, or until all of the stock has been absorbed.

2 Melt the butter in a small frying pan, add the garlic and onion and cook them over low heat for 5 minutes, or until they are softened. Add the onion mixture to the couscous with the parsley, coriander, pistachio nuts and 2 teaspoons of the spice mix, stir it together and season to taste. Cover the bowl with plastic wrap and keep it warm.

3 Put the yoghurt in a small bowl, stir in the lemon juice and honey, and season to taste.

4 Peel the pumpkin, cut it into 2 cm (^{3}/$_4$ inch) thick pieces and toss it in a bowl with the olive oil and the remaining spice mix. Preheat a covered or kettle barbecue to medium direct heat. Grill the pumpkin, covered, for 45 minutes, or until it is golden all over and cooked through. Pile the couscous onto a serving plate, top it with the grilled pumpkin pieces and serve with the yoghurt dressing.

❉ Note: Ras el hanout is a traditional Moroccan spice mix, and is available from gourmet food stores. The taste of this dish will rely on the quality of the spices used, so if you have time, make your own. Dry-fry 6 cardamom pods, ^{1}/$_2$ teaspoon black pepper and 1 teaspoon fennel seeds until they are fragrant. Let the spices cool, then grind them in a spice grinder or mortar and pestle and mix with ^{1}/$_2$ teaspoon ground cinnamon, 1 teaspoon turmeric, ^{1}/$_2$ teaspoon cayenne pepper, 2 teaspoons mild paprika, 1 teaspoon ground cumin, ^{1}/$_2$ teaspoon allspice and 1 teaspoon salt. The spice mix can be stored in an airtight container for up to 2 months.

SNAPPER ENVELOPE WITH GINGER AND SPRING ONIONS

DRESSING

1 spring onion (scallion)

3 tablespoons coriander (cilantro) leaves

1 teaspoon finely grated fresh ginger

2 tablespoons lime juice

1 tablespoon fish sauce

1/2 teaspoon sesame oil

1 whole snapper (about 1.8–2 kg/
    4 lb–4 lb 8 oz)

sea salt

1 lime

4 spring onions (scallions)

30 g (1 cup) coriander (cilantro) leaves

1 tablespoon finely grated fresh ginger

canola oil spray

SUITABLE FOR A COVERED BARBECUE
COOKING TIME: 20 MINUTES
SERVES 4

1 To make the dressing, finely slice the green part of the spring onion and the coriander leaves, and mix them together with the ginger, lime juice, fish sauce and sesame oil.

2 Check that the fish has been thoroughly scaled, then wash it under cold running water and pat it dry with paper towels. In the thickest part of the flesh make diagonal cuts 1.5 cm (5/8 inch) apart in one direction, then in the other direction, so that the flesh is scored in a diamond pattern. Lightly season the fish with sea salt and freshly ground black pepper.

3 Peel the lime, removing all the pith, with a small, sharp knife and separate the lime sections by carefully cutting each piece away from the membrane. Slice the spring onions on the diagonal, mix them with the coriander leaves, lime segments and ginger, and stuff the mixture into the cavity of the fish.

4 Lightly spray a double layer of foil with canola oil, making sure it is large enough to wrap around the fish and totally enclose it. Fold the foil around the fish and seal the edges tightly.

5 Preheat a kettle or covered barbecue to medium indirect heat. Put the fish in the middle of the barbecue and cook it, covered, for 10 minutes. Use a large metal spatula to turn the fish so that it will brown evenly on both sides and cook it for another 8–10 minutes, or until it flakes when tested in the thickest part of the flesh.

6 When the fish is cooked, open the foil envelope and slide it onto a serving plate. Pour the cooking juices over the fish, drizzle the dressing over the top and serve straight away. It is delicious with steamed jasmine rice and a green salad.

LAMB BURGER

1 tablespoon ground cumin

250 g (1 cup) plain Greek-style yoghurt

½ Lebanese (short) cucumber, grated

1 tablespoon finely chopped mint leaves

1 tablespoon olive oil

1 onion, finely chopped

2 garlic cloves, crushed

800 g (1 lb 12 oz) minced (ground) lamb

2 tablespoons finely chopped flat-leaf
    (Italian) parsley

2 tablespoons finely chopped coriander
    (cilantro) leaves

2 red capsicums (peppers), quartered and
    seeded

1 tablespoon olive oil, extra

2 red onions, thinly sliced

olive oil spray

1 loaf Turkish bread, cut into 4 pieces and
    split horizontally

100 g (4 handfuls) baby rocket (arugula)
    leaves

SUITABLE FOR A FLAT OR RIDGED
    GRILL PLATE
COOKING TIME: 15 MINUTES
SERVES 4

1 Dry-fry 1 teaspoon ground cumin over medium heat for 30 seconds, or until it is fragrant. Put the yoghurt, cucumber, mint and dry-fried cumin in a small bowl and mix it all together. Cover the bowl and refrigerate it until needed.

2 Heat the oil in a frying pan and cook the onion over medium heat for 2–3 minutes or until it is softened. Add the garlic and remaining cumin, cook it for another minute, then allow the mixture to cool. Put the onion mixture in a large bowl with the mince, parsley and coriander, season with salt and pepper and mix it together with your hands. Divide the mixture into four portions, and shape each portion into a 2 cm (³/4 inch) thick patty.

3 Heat the barbecue to medium–high direct heat. Toss the capsicum with the extra oil and cook it on the flat plate for 6 minutes on each side or until it is softened and lightly charred. Grill the lamb patties on the flat plate for 5–6 minutes each side or until they are done.

4 Spray the red onion with the olive oil spray and cook it on the flat plate for 2–3 minutes or until it is soft and golden. Toast the bread, cut side down, on the chargrill plate for 1–2 minutes or until it is marked and golden.

5 To assemble the burgers, put some rocket on four of the bread slices. Put a pattie on top, then the capsicum and onion. Dollop 2–3 tablespoons of the yoghurt mixture on each and season with salt and freshly ground black pepper, then top with the remaining bread slices and serve them straight away.

BEEF WITH BLUE CHEESE BUTTER AND PEAR AND WALNUT SALAD

100 g (3½ oz) butter, softened

2 garlic cloves, crushed

100 g (3½ oz) Blue Castello cheese

2 teaspoons finely shredded sage leaves

1 kg (2 lb 4 oz) beef eye fillet (thick end), trimmed

1 tablespoon olive oil

PEAR AND WALNUT SALAD

60 ml (¼ cup) walnut oil

1¼ tablespoons sherry vinegar

1 teaspoon Dijon mustard

3 ripe pears, halved, cored, cut into
    1 cm (½ inch) thick wedges

50 g (1¾ oz) butter, melted

1 tablespoon brown sugar

2 heads witlof (chicory/Belgian endive),
    leaves separated

85 g (⅔ cup) walnut pieces, toasted,
    chopped

SUITABLE FOR A FLAT OR RIDGED
    GRILL PLATE
COOKING TIME: 15 MINUTES
SERVES 4

1 To make the blue cheese butter, mash together the softened butter, garlic, cheese and sage until they are well combined. Form the mixture into a log and wrap it in baking paper, twisting the ends to seal them. Refrigerate the butter until firm, then cut it into 5 mm (¼ inch) slices and leave it at room temperature until needed.

2 To make the salad dressing, whisk the walnut oil, vinegar, mustard and some freshly ground black pepper in a bowl. Put the pears, melted butter and sugar in a bowl and toss them together until the pears are well coated in the butter.

3 Cut the beef into four thick, equal pieces and tie a piece of string around the edge of each so it will keep its shape during cooking. Brush both sides of each steak with the oil and season with freshly ground black pepper. Heat the barbecue to medium–high direct heat and cook the beef on the chargrill plate for 6–7 minutes on each side for medium, or to your liking. Cook the pear slices on the flat plate for 1 minute each side or until they are golden and slightly caramelized, basting with the butter and sugar mixture during cooking.

4 Put two slices of blue cheese butter on top of each steak as soon as you remove it from the barbecue and remove the string. Put the witlof in a large bowl, add the dressing, walnuts and pears and toss well, then serve the salad with the beef medallions.

✳ Note: Any leftover butter can be wrapped in baking paper and foil, and frozen for up to 2 months for later use. It is also delicious with chicken and pork.

HONEY-ROASTED PORK FILLET WITH PARSLEY CARROTS

1 tablespoon finely grated fresh ginger

6 garlic cloves

80 ml (1/3 cup) soy sauce

2 tablespoons oil

2 kg (4 lb 8 oz) piece pork neck or
   blade roast

2 tablespoons honey

PARSLEY CARROTS

600 g (1 lb 5 oz) baby carrots

2 teaspoons olive oil

30 g (1 oz) butter

2 tablespoons finely chopped flat-leaf
   (Italian) parsley

SUITABLE FOR A COVERED BARBECUE
COOKING TIME: 45 MINUTES
SERVES 6–8

1   Mix the ginger, garlic, soy sauce and oil in a large, non-metallic bowl.
    Put the pork in the marinade and turn it so that it is well coated, then
    cover the bowl and refrigerate it overnight.

2   Bring a saucepan of salted water to the boil, and blanch the carrots
    for 3 minutes or until they start to soften. Drain and refresh them
    under cold water and pat them dry with paper towels. Just before
    the pork is due to be ready, toss the carrots in olive oil and season
    them with salt and pepper.

3   Remove the pork from the marinade, pour the marinade into a small
    saucepan and simmer it over low heat for 5 minutes or until it is
    slightly reduced. Stir the honey into the warm marinade and remove
    it from the heat. Preheat a kettle or covered barbecue to low–medium
    indirect heat, then put the pork in the middle of the barbecue and
    roast it, covered, for 45 minutes or until it is cooked through. In the
    last 10 minutes of cooking, baste the roast all over with the reduced
    marinade. Be careful not to let any of the marinade splash onto the
    grill, as it may burn and stick. Remove the roast from the barbecue
    and put it on a tray, covered, to rest for 10 minutes.

4   While the roast is resting, cook the carrots on the chargrill plate for
    5 minutes, or until they are charred and golden all over, then toss the
    carrots with the butter and parsley until they are well coated. Season
    to taste with salt and freshly ground black pepper.

5   Carve the roast and serve it with any pan juices left in the tray and
    the warm parsley carrots.

73

TERIYAKI BABY OCTOPUS

125 ml (½ cup) sake
125 ml (½ cup) mirin
125 ml (½ cup) dark soy sauce
1 tablespoon caster (superfine) sugar
2 teaspoons grated fresh ginger
2 garlic cloves, finely chopped
1 kg (2 lb 4 oz) baby octopus

SUITABLE FOR A FLAT OR RIDGED
   GRILL PLATE
COOKING TIME: 10 MINUTES
SERVES 4

1 Combine the sake, mirin, dark soy sauce and sugar in a small saucepan. Bring the mixture to the boil over medium heat and boil, stirring until all the sugar has dissolved, then add the ginger and garlic and remove the saucepan from the heat. Leave the mixture to cool for 30 minutes.

2 Meanwhile, to prepare the octopus, use a small knife to carefully cut between the head and tentacles of the octopus, just below the eyes. Push the beak out and up through the tentacles with your finger, then remove the eyes from the head of the octopus by cutting off a small disc and discarding it. To clean the octopus tube, carefully slit through one side, avoiding the ink sac, and scrape out any gut. Rinse the inside under running water to remove any remaining gut and cut it in half. Wash the rest of the octopus thoroughly under running water, pulling the skin away from the tube and tentacles. If the octopus are large, cut the tentacles into quarters.

3 Put the octopus in a large, non-metallic bowl. Whisk the teriyaki marinade, making sure that it is well combined, then pour it over the octopus, stirring so that the octopus is thoroughly coated. Cover and marinate it in the refrigerator for at least 2 hours, or overnight.

4 Preheat the chargrill plate to medium direct heat. Remove the octopus from the teriyaki marinade and cook them for 2–3 minutes, or until they are cooked through, curled and glazed. Arrange the octopus on top of the Asian salad to serve.

ASIAN SALAD

2 sheets nori, cut into 3 cm x 5 mm
   (1 1/4 x 1/4 inch) pieces
2 tablespoons seasoned rice wine
   vinegar
2 teaspoons lemon juice
1/4 teaspoon sesame oil
2 teaspoons canola oil
60 g (2 1/4 oz) mizuna leaves
60 g (2 1/4 oz) snow pea shoots
2 Lebanese (short) cucumbers, shaved
1/2 daikon, shaved

Toast the nori on a preheated
barbecue plate for 5 minutes to
make it crispy. Make the dressing
by whisking together the rice wine
vinegar, lemon juice, sesame oil and
canola oil. Toss the mizuna, snow
pea shoots, cucumber, daikon and
nori with the dressing, and serve
the salad with the octopus.

LEBANESE CHICKEN WITH EGGPLANT, TOMATO AND SUMAC SALAD

250 g (1 cup) plain Greek-style yoghurt

2 teaspoons brown sugar

4 garlic cloves, crushed

3 teaspoons ground cumin

1½ teaspoons ground coriander

7 g (¼ cup) chopped flat-leaf (Italian)
   parsley

60 ml (¼ cup) lemon juice

1 x 1.8 kg (4 lb) chicken, cut into
   10 serving pieces

cooking oil spray

EGGPLANT, TOMATO AND SUMAC SALAD

2 eggplants (aubergines), cut into
   1 cm (½ inch) thick rounds

100 ml (5 tablespoons) olive oil

5 large ripe tomatoes

1 small red onion, finely sliced

20 g (⅓ cup) roughly chopped mint leaves

10 g (⅓ cup) roughly chopped flat-leaf
   (Italian) parsley

2 teaspoons sumac (see Note)

2 tablespoons lemon juice

SUITABLE FOR ANY BARBECUE
COOKING TIME: 40 MINUTES
SERVES 6

1 Put the yoghurt, brown sugar, garlic, cumin, coriander, chopped parsley and lemon juice in a large, non-metallic bowl and mix them together. Add the chicken pieces to the marinade and turn them so that they are completely coated, then cover and refrigerate for at least 2 hours, or overnight.

2 To make the eggplant, tomato and sumac salad, put the eggplant slices in a colander, and sprinkle them with salt. Leave the eggplant for 30 minutes to allow some of the bitter juices to drain away, then rinse the slices and pat them dry with paper towels. Brush both sides of each slice with 2 tablespoons of the olive oil, then chargrill them for 5 minutes on each side or until they are cooked through. Let the slices cool slightly and cut them in half.

3 Cut the tomatoes into wedges and arrange them in a serving bowl with the eggplant and onion. Scatter the mint, parsley and sumac over the top, then put the lemon juice and remaining olive oil in a small, screw-top jar, season, and shake it up. Drizzle the dressing over the salad and toss it gently.

4 Lightly spray the barbecue plates with oil, then preheat the barbecue to medium direct heat. Take the chicken pieces out of the marinade and season them with salt and pepper. Cook the chicken pieces on the flat plate, turning them frequently, for 20–30 minutes, or until they are cooked through. If you have a barbecue with a lid, cover the barbecue while the chicken is cooking. This way, the breast pieces will take only 15 minutes to cook, while the pieces on the bone will take about 10 minutes longer. Serve the chicken with the eggplant, tomato and sumac salad.

✳ Note: Sumac is a spice made from crushing the dried sumac berry. It has a mild lemony flavour and is used extensively in many cuisines, from North Africa and the Middle East, to India and Asia.

MARINATED VEGETABLE SALAD WITH BABY BOCCONCINI
AND PESTO DRESSING

2 large red capsicums (peppers), cored
  and seeded
5 slender eggplants (aubergines), cut into
  1 cm (1/2 inch) slices on the diagonal
300 g (10 1/2 oz) asparagus spears, trimmed
  and halved
4 zucchini (courgettes), cut into 1 cm
  (1/2 inch) slices on the diagonal
300 g (10 1/2 oz) small field mushrooms,
  quartered
125 ml (1/2 cup) olive oil
4 garlic cloves, crushed
200 g (7 oz) bocconcini, sliced
150 g (5 1/2 oz) baby rocket (arugula) leaves
1 tablespoon balsamic vinegar

PESTO
40 g (2 cups) small basil leaves
50 g (1/3 cup) pine nuts, toasted
3 garlic cloves, crushed
1/2 teaspoon sea salt
125 ml (1/2 cup) olive oil
20 g (1/2 oz) Parmesan cheese, finely grated
20 g (1/2 oz) pecorino cheese, finely grated

SUITABLE FOR A FLAT OR RIDGED
  GRILL PLATE
COOKING TIME: 10 MINUTES
SERVES 4

1 Cut the capsicums into quarters, then each quarter into three strips. Put the capsicum, eggplant, asparagus, zucchini and mushrooms in a large bowl, pour in the combined oil and garlic, season with salt and freshly ground pepper, and toss it all together. Leave the vegetables to marinate for 1 hour, tossing occasionally.

2 To make the pesto, put the basil, pine nuts, garlic, salt and oil in a food processor and process until it is smooth. Stir in the Parmesan and pecorino, then cover the bowl until you are ready to use it.

3 Heat the flat plate to high and cook the vegetables, turning, for 7–8 minutes, or until they are soft and golden. Arrange the grilled vegetables on a serving plate with the bocconcini, and toss the rocket with the vinegar. Drizzle the vegetables with the pesto and serve them immediately with warmed, crusty bread rolls.

THAI BEEF SALAD

80 ml (1/3 cup) lime juice

2 tablespoons fish sauce

2 teaspoons grated palm sugar or soft
brown sugar

1 garlic clove, crushed

1 tablespoon finely chopped coriander
(cilantro) roots and stems

1 stem lemon grass (white part only), finely
chopped

2 small red chillies, finely sliced

2 x 200 g (7 oz) beef eye fillet steaks

150 g (5 1/2 oz) mixed salad leaves

1/2 red onion, cut into thin wedges

15 g (1/2 cup) coriander (cilantro) leaves

7 g (1/3 cup) torn mint leaves

250 g (9 oz) cherry tomatoes, halved

1 Lebanese (short) cucumber, halved
lengthways and thinly sliced on the
diagonal

SUITABLE FOR ANY BARBECUE
COOKING TIME: 10 MINUTES
SERVES 4

1 Mix together the lime juice, fish sauce, palm sugar, garlic, chopped coriander, lemon grass and chilli until the sugar has dissolved.

2 Preheat the chargrill plate to medium–high direct heat and cook the steaks for 4 minutes on each side, or until medium. Let the steaks cool, then slice them thinly across the grain.

3 Put the salad leaves, onion, coriander leaves, mint, tomatoes and cucumber in a large bowl, add the beef and dressing, toss them together and serve immediately.

SAGE AND RICOTTA STUFFED CHICKEN WITH BABY SPINACH

250 g (1 cup) fresh ricotta cheese, well
 drained

1 tablespoon shredded sage leaves

2 garlic cloves, crushed

1½ teaspoons lemon zest

40 g (1½ oz) finely grated Parmesan
 cheese

4 chicken breast fillets, tenderloin removed

8 thin slices prosciutto

olive oil, for brushing

BABY SPINACH SALAD

150 g (5½ oz) baby spinach leaves

100 g (3½ oz) small black olives

2 tablespoons olive oil

1 tablespoon lemon juice

sea salt

SUITABLE FOR A FLAT OR RIDGED
 GRILL PLATE

COOKING TIME: 15 MINUTES

SERVES 4

1 Mix together the ricotta, sage, garlic, zest and Parmesan until they are well combined. Use a sharp knife to cut a large pocket into the side of each chicken breast and fill each pocket with a quarter of the ricotta mixture. Pin the pockets closed with toothpicks and wrap each breast in two slices of prosciutto, securing it with a toothpick.

2 To make the spinach salad, toss the spinach in a large serving bowl with the olives and the combined olive oil and lemon juice. Season the salad with sea salt and freshly ground black pepper.

3 Heat the flat plate to medium direct heat, brush the chicken parcels with olive oil and season them with freshly ground black pepper. Cook them for 8 minutes on each side, or until they are cooked through. Serve the chicken with the salad.

PORK AND FENNEL SAUSAGES WITH ONION RELISH

750 g (1 lb 10 oz) minced (ground) pork

40 g (1/2 cup) fresh breadcrumbs

2 garlic cloves, crushed

3 teaspoons fennel seeds, coarsely crushed

1 teaspoon finely grated orange zest

2 teaspoons chopped thyme leaves

7 g (1/4 cup) chopped flat-leaf (Italian)
  parsley

oil, for brushing

1 long baguette, cut into 4 pieces, or
  4 long, crusty rolls

50 g (1 3/4 oz) butter, softened

60 g (2 1/4 oz) rocket (arugula) leaves

1 tablespoon extra virgin olive oil

1 teaspoon balsamic vinegar

ONION RELISH

50 g (1 3/4 oz) butter

2 red onions, thinly sliced

1 tablespoon soft brown sugar

2 tablespoons balsamic vinegar

SUITABLE FOR A FLAT OR RIDGED
  GRILL PLATE
COOKING TIME: 1 HOUR
MAKES 8

1 Put the mince, breadcrumbs, garlic, fennel seeds, zest, thyme and parsley in a large bowl, season well with salt and freshly ground black pepper and mix it all together with your hands. Cover the mixture and refrigerate it for 4 hours or overnight.

2 To make the onion relish, melt the butter in a heavy-based saucepan, add the onion and cook, stirring occasionally, over low heat for 10 minutes, or until the onion is softened, but not browned. Add the brown sugar and vinegar, and continue to cook it for another 30 minutes, stirring regularly.

3 Preheat the flat plate to medium direct heat. Divide the pork mixture into eight portions and use wet hands to mould each portion into a flattish sausage shape. Lightly brush the sausages with oil and cook them for 8 minutes on each side, or until they are cooked through.

4 To assemble, split the rolls down the middle and butter them. Toss the rocket with the olive oil and balsamic vinegar, and put some of the leaves in each of the rolls. Top with a sausage and a some of the onion relish.

LAMB STUFFED WITH OLIVES, FETA AND OREGANO

85 g (½ cup) Kalamata olives, pitted
3 garlic cloves, crushed
100 ml (5 tablespoons) olive oil
800 g (1 lb 12 oz) lamb sirloin, trimmed
 (see Note)
90 g (3¼ oz) feta cheese, crumbled
2 tablespoons oregano leaves, finely
 shredded
80 ml (⅓ cup) lemon juice

SUITABLE FOR ANY BARBECUE
COOKING TIME: 10 MINUTES
SERVES 4

1 Put the Kalamata olives in a food processor or blender with the garlic and 2 tablespoons of olive oil, and blend until it is smooth. Season to taste with freshly ground black pepper.

2 Prepare the sirloin by cutting horizontally most of the way through the piece, starting at one end, leaving a small join at the other end. Open out the lamb so you have a piece half as thick and twice as long as you started with.

3 Spread the olive and garlic paste in a thin, even layer over the cut surface of the lamb, then crumble the feta over the top and scatter with the chopped oregano. Roll the lamb tightly, starting with one of the long cut edges, and tie the whole length with cooking twine, so that the filling is contained and secure.

4 Put the lamb into a dish large enough to hold it lying flat and drizzle it with the lemon juice and remaining olive oil, turning to make sure that all of the lamb is well coated. Cover the dish and refrigerate it for 3 hours.

5 Prepare a chargrill plate to medium—high direct heat. Season the lamb and grill it, turning to brown each side, for 10 minutes, or until it is cooked to your liking. Remove it from the barbecue and let it rest, covered, for 5 minutes. Use a very sharp knife to cut the roll into 5 cm (2 inch) pieces on the diagonal and serve it immediately with a mixed green salad.

✳ Note: Use the thick end of the sirloin for this recipe.

SMOKED TROUT WITH LEMON AND DILL BUTTER

LEMON AND DILL BUTTER
125 g (4½ oz) butter, softened
2 tablespoons lemon juice
2 tablespoons finely chopped dill
½ teaspoon lemon zest
1 small garlic clove, crushed

6 hickory woodchips
4 rainbow trout
oil, for brushing

SUITABLE FOR A KETTLE BARBECUE
COOKING TIME: 15 MINUTES
SERVES 4

1   Mash together the butter, lemon juice, dill, zest and garlic, shape it into a log and wrap it in greaseproof paper, twisting the ends to seal them. Refrigerate the butter until it is firm, then cut it into 1 cm (½ inch) slices and leave it at room temperature.

2   Preheat a kettle barbecue to low indirect heat, allow the coals to burn down to ash, then add three hickory woodchips to each side.

3   Brush the skin of the fish with oil. When the woodchips begin to smoke, put the trout on the barbecue, replace the cover and smoke them for 15 minutes or until they are cooked through. Remove the fish from the grill, gently peel off the skin and top them with the lemon and dill butter while they are still hot. Smoked trout are delicious with boiled new potatoes and a green salad, and can also be served cold.

Note: Like barbecuing, smoking is a simple process with a delicious result. Special woodchips are commercially available which will give off a wonderfully scented smoke and infuse your food with a distinctive flavour. Never use wood that is not specifically intended for smoking food, as many woods are chemically treated and may make the food poisonous. To smoke food, soak six woodchips in water for 1 hour and prepare a kettle barbecue for indirect cooking. When the briquettes are ready, add three woodchips to each side and close the lid until the chips begin to smoke, then cook the food according to the recipe, lifting the lid as little as possible so you don't lose too much of the smoke. Smoking does not work in a gas or electric barbecue as the chips need to burn to infuse their aromatic flavour.

SATAY CHICKEN

500 g (1 lb 2 oz) chicken thigh fillets, cut
   into 1 cm (1/2 inch) wide strips
1 garlic clove, crushed
2 teaspoons finely grated fresh ginger
3 teaspoons fish sauce

SATAY SAUCE
2 teaspoons peanut oil
4 red Asian shallots, finely chopped
4 garlic cloves, crushed
2 teaspoons finely chopped fresh ginger
2 small red chillies, seeded and finely
   chopped
125 g (1/2 cup) crunchy peanut butter
185 ml (3/4 cup) coconut milk
2 teaspoons soy sauce
2 teaspoons grated palm sugar or soft
   brown sugar
1 1/2 tablespoons fish sauce
1 fresh kaffir (makrut) lime leaf
1 1/2 tablespoons lime juice

SUITABLE FOR A FLAT OR RIDGED
   GRILL PLATE
COOKING TIME: 25 MINUTES
SERVES 4

1 Put the chicken, garlic, ginger and fish sauce in a bowl and turn
the chicken so that it is well coated. Cover the bowl and leave it
in the refrigerator for 1 hour. Soak 12 wooden skewers in cold water
for 1 hour.

2 To make the satay sauce, heat the oil in a saucepan over medium
heat, then add the shallot, garlic, ginger and chilli. Stir the mixture
constantly with a wooden spoon for 5 minutes, or until the shallots
are golden. Reduce the heat to low, add the remaining sauce
ingredients and simmer for 10 minutes, or until the sauce has
thickened. Remove the lime leaf and keep the sauce warm while
you cook the chicken.

3 Preheat the chargrill plate to medium–high direct heat. Thread two
or three chicken strips onto each skewer, without crowding them,
and grill the chicken for 10 minutes, or until it is cooked through,
turning after 5 minutes. Serve the skewers with the satay sauce
and cucumber salad.

CUCUMBER SALAD

1 telegraph (long) cucumber

1 tablespoon sugar

60 ml (¼ cup) lime juice

1 tablespoon fish sauce

1 red Asian shallot, finely sliced

10 g (⅓ cup) coriander (cilantro)
 leaves

1 small red chilli, seeds removed and
 finely chopped

75 g (2½ oz) snow pea shoots

Peel the cucumber, cut it in half
lengthways, remove the seeds and
cut it into 5 mm (¼ inch) slices. Put
the sugar and lime juice in a large
bowl, and stir them together until
the sugar has dissolved, then add
the fish sauce. Toss the cucumber,
shallot, coriander and chilli through
the dressing, cover and refrigerate
for 15 minutes. Just before serving,
cut the snow pea shoots in half and
stir them through the salad.

HOISIN LAMB WITH CHARRED SPRING ONION AND ASIAN RICE SALAD

800 g (1 lb 12 oz) lamb loin

60 ml (¼ cup) hoisin sauce

2 tablespoons soy sauce

2 garlic cloves, bruised

1 tablespoon grated fresh ginger

2 teaspoons olive oil

16 spring onions (scallions), trimmed to
    18 cm (7 inches) long

40 g (¼ cup) chopped toasted peanuts

ASIAN RICE SALAD

400 g (2 cups) long-grain rice

2 tablespoons olive oil

1 large red onion, finely chopped

4 garlic cloves, crushed

1 tablespoon finely chopped fresh ginger

1 long red chilli, seeded and thinly sliced

4 spring onions (scallions), finely sliced

2 tablespoons soy sauce

½ teaspoon sesame oil

2 teaspoons black vinegar (see Note)

1 tablespoon lime juice

50 g (1 cup) roughly chopped coriander
    (cilantro) leaves

SUITABLE FOR A FLAT OR RIDGED
    GRILL PLATE
COOKING TIME: 35 MINUTES
SERVES 4

1 Trim the lamb of any excess fat and sinew. Combine the hoisin sauce, soy sauce, garlic, ginger and 1 teaspoon of the oil in a shallow dish, add the lamb and turn it so that it is well coated in the marinade. Cover the dish and refrigerate for 4 hours or overnight.

2 To make the rice salad, bring 1.25 litres (5 cups) of water to the boil in a large saucepan. Add the rice and cook it, uncovered, for 12–15 minutes over low heat, or until the grains are tender. Drain and rinse the rice under cold running water, then transfer it to a large bowl. While the rice is cooking, heat the oil in a frying pan over medium heat. Add the onion, garlic, ginger and chilli, and cook them for 5–6 minutes, or until the onion has softened, but not browned. Stir in the spring onion and cook for another minute. Remove the onion mixture from the heat and add it to the rice with the soy sauce, sesame oil, vinegar, lime juice and coriander, and mix well. Cover the rice salad and refrigerate until you are ready to serve.

3 Toss the trimmed spring onions with the remaining oil and season them well. Remove the lamb from the marinade, season the meat and pour the marinade into a small saucepan. Simmer the marinade for 5 minutes, or until it is slightly reduced. Preheat the chargrill plate to medium direct heat. Cook the lamb for 5–6 minutes on each side, or until it is cooked to your liking, brushing it frequently with the reduced marinade, then let it rest, covered, for 3 minutes. Grill the spring onions for 1–2 minutes, or until they are tender, but still firm.

4 Cut the lamb across the grain into 2 cm (¾ inch) thick slices, and arrange it on a serving plate. Drizzle any juices that have been released during resting over the lamb and sprinkle it with the toasted peanuts. Serve with the spring onions and rice salad.

 Note: Black vinegar is a type of Chinese vinegar and can be found in Asian grocery stores.

PORK LOIN WITH APPLE GLAZE, DILL COLESLAW AND WEDGES

COLESLAW

90 g (1/3 cup) sour cream

2 teaspoons prepared horseradish

1 tablespoon lemon juice

1 tablespoon Dijon mustard

2 tablespoons finely chopped dill

300 g (4 cups) shredded red cabbage

2 carrots, peeled and grated

1 teaspoon aniseed

135 g (1/2 cup) apple sauce

2 tablespoons brown sugar

1.5 kg (3 lb 5 oz) boned pork loin with
the skin on

2 teaspoons oil

4 large potatoes, each cut into 8 wedges

2 tablespoons olive oil

2 teaspoons garlic salt

SUITABLE FOR A COVERED BARBECUE
COOKING TIME: 1 HOUR 5 MINUTES
SERVES 6–8

1 To make the coleslaw, put the sour cream, horseradish, lemon juice, mustard and dill in a large bowl and stir it together. Add the cabbage and carrot, toss them together well so that the coleslaw is lightly coated with dressing, and season to taste.

2 Dry-fry the aniseed over medium heat for 30 seconds, or until it becomes fragrant, then add the apple sauce and brown sugar, reduce the heat to low and cook, stirring, for 1 minute.

3 Use a sharp knife to carefully remove the skin from the pork loin. Score the skin in a diamond pattern and rub the oil and 1 tablespoon of salt over the skin, working it into the cuts. Put the potato wedges in a bowl with the olive oil and garlic salt, season them well with black pepper and toss until the wedges are well coated in oil.

4 Preheat a kettle or covered barbecue to medium indirect heat. Tie the pork loin with string to help it keep its shape, then put the pork and the skin in the barbecue and arrange the wedges around them. After 30 minutes, baste the pork with the apple glaze, and repeat every 10 minutes for another 30 minutes (for 1 hour cooking time in all). Turn the skin and the wedges as you go so that they cook evenly.

5 When the pork is ready, remove it from the barbecue and leave to rest, covered, for 10 minutes before carving. Cut the crackling with a sharp knife and arrange it on a serving platter with the pork and serve it with the wedges and coleslaw.

STUFFED BABY CALAMARI WITH LIME AND CHILLI DIPPING SAUCE

DIPPING SAUCE

80 ml (1/3 cup) lime juice

60 ml (1/4 cup) fish sauce

2 tablespoons grated palm sugar or soft
  brown sugar

1 small red chilli, finely sliced into rounds

12 medium squid

12 raw prawns (shrimp), peeled, deveined
  and chopped

150 g (5 1/2 oz) minced (ground) pork

4 garlic cloves, crushed

1/2 teaspoon finely grated fresh ginger

3 teaspoons fish sauce

2 teaspoons lime juice

1 teaspoon grated palm sugar

2 tablespoons chopped coriander (cilantro)
  leaves

peanut oil, for brushing

SUITABLE FOR A FLAT OR RIDGED
  GRILL PLATE

COOKING TIME: 10 MINUTES

SERVES 4

1 To make the dipping sauce, put the lime juice, fish sauce, palm sugar and chilli in a small bowl and stir it all together until the sugar has dissolved. Cover the bowl and leave it until you are ready to eat.

2 Gently pull the tentacles away from the tube of the squid (the intestines should come away at the same time). Remove the quill from inside the body and throw it away, as well as any white membrane. Pull the skin away from the hood under cold running water, then cut the tentacles away from the intestines and give them a good rinse to remove the sucker rings. Finely chop the tentacles and keep them to add to the stuffing.

3 Put the prawns, pork, garlic, ginger, fish sauce, lime juice, palm sugar, coriander and chopped tentacles in a bowl and mix them together. Use a teaspoon to put some of the stuffing in each tube and push it to the bottom, then secure the hole with a toothpick. Take care to not overfill the tubes as the stuffing will expand when you cook them.

4 Preheat the chargrill plate to medium direct heat, brush the squid tubes with peanut oil, and barbecue them for 8 minutes, or until they are cooked through, turning them when the flesh becomes opaque and slightly charred. Remove the tubes from the grill, take out the toothpicks and cut each tube into 1 cm (1/2 inch) rounds. Serve with the dipping sauce.

CHARGRILLED VEGETABLES WITH BASIL AIOLI

BASIL AIOLI

1 garlic clove

15 g (1/4 cup) torn basil leaves

1 egg yolk

125 ml (1/2 cup) olive oil

2 teaspoons lemon juice

2 large red capsicums (peppers), quartered,
    core and seeds removed

1 eggplant (aubergine), cut in 5 mm
    (1/4 inch) thick rounds

1 orange sweet potato, peeled and cut on
    the diagonal into 5 mm (1/4 inch) thick
    rounds

3 zucchini (courgettes), sliced lengthways
    into 5 mm (1/4 inch) thick slices

2 red onions, cut into 1 cm (1/2 inch) thick
    rounds

80 ml (1/3 cup) olive oil

1 loaf Turkish bread, split and cut into
    4 equal pieces

SUITABLE FOR A FLAT OR RIDGED
    GRILL PLATE
COOKING TIME: 15 MINUTES
SERVES 4

1 To make the basil aïoli, put the garlic, basil and egg yolk in the bowl of a food processor and blend them until they are smooth. With the motor running, gradually add the oil in a thin stream until the mixture thickens, then stir in the lemon juice and season to taste. Cover and refrigerate until you are ready to dish up.

2 Preheat the chargrill plate to medium direct heat. Put the capsicum, skin side down, around the cool edge of the grill and cook it for 8–10 minutes or until the skin has softened and is blistering.

3 Meanwhile, brush the eggplant, sweet potato, zucchini and onion slices on both sides with olive oil and season them lightly. Cook the vegetables in batches on the middle of the chargrill for 5–8 minutes, or until they are cooked through but still firm. As the vegetable pieces cook, put them on a tray in a single layer to prevent them from steaming, then grill the Turkish bread on both sides until it is lightly marked and toasted.

4 To assemble the burgers, spread both cut sides of the bread with 1 tablespoon of basil aïoli and pile on some of the chargrilled vegetables. Top with the remaining toast and serve immediately.

KOREAN BARBECUE BEEF IN LETTUCE LEAVES

600 g (1 lb 5 oz) sirloin steak

1 onion, grated

5 garlic cloves, crushed

125 ml (1/2 cup) Japanese soy sauce

1 teaspoon sesame oil

1 tablespoon oil

2 teaspoons finely grated fresh ginger

2 tablespoons brown sugar

1 tablespoon toasted sesame seeds, ground

1 butter lettuce

370 g (2 cups) cooked white rice

2 spring onions (scallions), finely sliced on the diagonal

2 small red chillies, sliced, or chilli sauce, optional

SUITABLE FOR A FLAT OR RIDGED GRILL PLATE

COOKING TIME: 1 MINUTE

SERVES: 4–6

1 Trim any excess fat from the steak then put it in the freezer for about 45 minutes, or until it is almost frozen through. Put the onion, garlic, soy sauce, oils, ginger, sugar, ground sesame seeds and 1 teaspoon of freshly ground black pepper in a large, non-metallic bowl and stir it all together well.

2 Using a very sharp, heavy knife cut the steak across the grain into 2–3 mm (1/8 inch) thick slices. Use a meat mallet or rolling pin to pound the meat until it is as thin as possible. Add the meat to the marinade and stir it to make sure that all of the meat is well coated in the marinade. Cover and refrigerate overnight.

3 Separate the lettuce leaves and put them in a large bowl with enough cold water to cover them and refrigerate.

4 Remove the meat and the lettuce from the refrigerator and drain the lettuce well or dry it in a salad spinner. Put the lettuce leaves, hot rice, spring onion and chilli in separate bowls and put them on the table ready for each person to serve themselves. Preheat the flat plate to high indirect heat and, working quickly, put the beef strips on the flat plate, spacing them out in a single layer, and cook them for about 10 seconds on each side. Do this in two batches if your barbecue isn't large enough to fit them all at once.

5 To make a wrap, put some rice in the bottom of a lettuce leaf, top it with a little meat, some spring onion and chilli if you like it, then wrap the leaf around the filling and eat it immediately.

ADOBO PORK WITH COCONUT RICE AND GRILLED MANGO

ADOBO PORK WITH COCONUT RICE

170 ml (²/₃ cup) balsamic vinegar
80 ml (¹/₃ cup) soy sauce
3 fresh bay leaves
4 garlic cloves, crushed
6 pork loin chops on the bone
2 tablespoons oil
lime wedges

COCONUT RICE

400 g (2 cups) jasmine rice
2 tablespoons oil
1 small onion, finely diced
1 teaspoon grated fresh ginger
2 garlic cloves, crushed
625 ml (2¹/₂ cups) coconut milk

SUITABLE FOR ANY BARBECUE
COOKING TIME: 40 MINUTES
SERVES 6

1 Put the balsamic vinegar, soy sauce, bay leaves, crushed garlic and ¹/₂ teaspoon freshly ground black pepper in a non-metallic dish and mix them all together. Add the pork chops to the marinade and turn them a few times so that they are thoroughly coated. Cover the bowl and refrigerate for at least 3 hours, or overnight.

2 To make the coconut rice, rinse the rice under cold, running water until the water runs clear. Heat the oil in a heavy-based saucepan over medium heat, then add the diced onion, ginger and garlic. Cook the mixture for 3 minutes, or until the onion has softened, then add the rice and stir for 1 minute, or until the rice is coated in oil. Stir in the coconut milk, bring it to the boil, then turn the heat down as low as possible and cook it very gently, covered, for 15 minutes. Remove the pan from the heat and let the rice sit for 5 minutes with the lid on, before gently fluffing it with a fork. Season well with salt and pepper.

3 Preheat the chargrill plate to medium direct heat. Remove the pork from the marinade and pat it dry with paper towels, then brush both sides of each chop with the oil and season them lightly with salt and pepper. Cook the chops for 8 minutes on each side, or until they are cooked through, then serve them with the coconut rice, grilled mango and lime wedges.

GRILLED MANGO

3 small mangoes
2 teaspoons oil

Preheat the barbecue to medium direct
heat. To prepare the mango, cut each
cheek straight down on either side
of the stone. Score the flesh without
cutting through the skin and lightly
brush the cut surface with the oil.
Cook the mango on the chargrill
plate, skin side down, for 2 minutes,
then turn it 90 degrees and cook for
another 2 minutes to make crossed
grill marks. Serve warm.

TANDOORI LAMB WITH MINTED POTATO SALAD AND SALSA

60 g (¼ cup) tandoori paste
250 g (1 cup) thick plain yoghurt
1 tablespoon lemon juice
4 racks of lamb with 4–5 cutlets in each

MINTED POTATO SALAD
600 g (1 lb 5 oz) chat potatoes, large ones
    halved
125 g (½ cup) thick plain yoghurt
1 Lebanese (short) cucumber, grated and
    squeezed dry
15 g (¼ cup) finely chopped mint leaves
2 garlic cloves, crushed

TOMATO AND ONION SALSA
6 Roma (plum) tomatoes
1 red onion
2 tablespoons lemon juice
1 teaspoon sugar
2 tablespoons olive oil

SUITABLE FOR A COVERED BARBECUE
COOKING TIME: 30 MINUTES
SERVES 4

1 Mix together the tandoori paste, yoghurt and the lemon juice in a large, non-metallic bowl. Trim any excess fat off the racks of lamb, add them to the marinade and turn them so that they are well coated. Cover and refrigerate for at least 4 hours, or overnight.

2 To make the minted potato salad, boil or steam the potatoes for 10 minutes, or until they are tender, then leave them to cool. Mix together the yoghurt, cucumber, mint and garlic and toss it through the potatoes. Season the potato salad well, cover the bowl, and refrigerate it until you are ready to dish up.

3 To make the tomato and onion salsa, cut the tomatoes into thin wedges, slice the onion very thinly and toss them both with the lemon juice, sugar and olive oil. Season the salsa with salt and lots of freshly cracked black pepper.

4 Preheat a kettle or covered barbecue to medium–high indirect heat. Cook the lamb, covered, for 10 minutes, then turn it, baste with the marinade and cook it for another 8 minutes. Leave it to rest, covered with foil, for 5 minutes. Serve the racks whole or sliced with the potato salad and tomato salsa.

SCALLOP AND FISH ROSEMARY SKEWERS WITH MARJORAM
DRESSING AND CHARGRILLED RADICCHIO SALAD

2 tablespoons marjoram leaves

1 tablespoon lemon juice

80 ml (1/3 cup) olive oil, plus extra, for
   brushing

7 g (1/4 cup) chopped flat-leaf (Italian)
   parsley

8 long firm rosemary branches

50 g (1 3/4 oz) rocket (arugula) leaves

600 g (1 lb 5 oz) firm white fish fillets, cut
   into 3 cm (1 1/4 inch) cubes

16 scallops with roe attached

2 heads radicchio, green outer leaves
   removed, cut into 8 wedges

lemon wedges

SUITABLE FOR A FLAT OR RIDGED
   GRILL PLATE

COOKING TIME: 10 MINUTES

SERVES 4

1   Pound the marjoram leaves in a mortar and pestle with a little salt, or very finely chop them until they become a paste. Add the lemon juice, then stir in the olive oil and parsley, and season to taste.

2   Pull the leaves off the rosemary branches, leaving just a tuft at the end of each stem. Thread three pieces of fish and two scallops alternately onto each rosemary skewer, brush them with a little olive oil and season well.

3   Preheat the flat plate to medium direct heat. Cook the skewers for 3–4 minutes on each side or until the fish is cooked through. While the skewers are cooking, add the radicchio to the plate in batches for 1–2 minutes on each side or until it is just wilted and slightly browned. Put the radicchio wedges on a tray in a single layer so that the leaves don't steam in their own heat.

4   Arrange the radicchio on a flat serving dish, gently combine it with the rocket and drizzle a little of the marjoram dressing across the top. Serve the skewers with the radicchio salad, lemon wedges and the extra dressing.

LAMB FILLETS WRAPPED IN VINE LEAVES WITH AVGOLEMONO SAUCE AND GRILLED POTATOES

12 lamb fillets (approximately 700 g/
   1 lb 9 oz)
2 teaspoons lemon juice
1 1/2 teaspoons ground cumin
2 tablespoons olive oil
1 kg (2 lb 4 oz) waxy potatoes
   (e.g. pink fir apple, kipfler)
12 large vine leaves preserved in brine

AVGOLEMONO SAUCE
2 eggs
1 egg yolk
60 ml (1/4 cup) lemon juice
100 ml (5 tablespoons) chicken stock

SUITABLE FOR A FLAT OR RIDGED
   GRILL PLATE
COOKING TIME: 30 MINUTES
SERVES 4

1 Trim the fillets and put them in a bowl with the lemon juice, cumin and 1 tablespoon of the olive oil, then turn the fillets so they are coated. Cover the bowl and leave the lamb to marinate for 1 hour. Steam or boil the potatoes for 10–15 minutes or until they are just tender, and when they are cool enough to handle, peel them and slice each one in half lengthways. Toss the potato halves gently in the remaining olive oil, and season.

2 Rinse the vine leaves under warm water, pat them dry with paper towels and remove any woody stems. Lay the leaf flat with the vein side facing up, remove the lamb from the marinade, season it well with salt and pepper, and put a lamb fillet on the bottom of each vine leaf. Roll up the leaf so that it is wrapped around the lamb with the join sitting underneath.

3 To make the avgolemono sauce, whisk the whole eggs, egg yolk and lemon juice together, then bring the chicken stock to the boil and add 1 tablespoon of the hot stock to the egg mixture. Mix them together, then slowly add the egg mixture to the stock, stirring continuously. Cook the sauce over low heat, stirring it constantly with a wooden spoon for 4–5 minutes, or until it thickens enough to hold a line drawn across the back of the spoon. Be very careful to not let the sauce boil, or the mixture will curdle beyond redemption.

4 Preheat a barbecue to medium direct heat. Cook the potatoes on the chargrill plate for 6–7 minutes, or until they are golden and crisp and the lamb fillets for 1–2 minutes on each side for medium–rare, or until they are done to your liking.

5 Slice the lamb fillets in half on the diagonal and serve them with the sauce and grilled potatoes.

YAKITORI CHICKEN BURGER

4 chicken thigh fillets, trimmed

185 ml (3/4 cup) yakitori sauce

1 teaspoon cornflour

oil, for brushing

4 soft hamburger buns, halved

80 g (1/3 cup) Japanese mayonnaise
  (see Note)

80 g (2 handfuls) mizuna lettuce

1 Lebanese (short) cucumber, ends
  trimmed and shaved into ribbons with
  a vegetable peeler

SUITABLE FOR ANY BARBECUE
COOKING TIME: 20 MINUTES
SERVES 4

1 Toss the chicken and yakitori sauce together in a bowl until the chicken is well coated, then cover and refrigerate for 4 hours.

2 Drain the yakitori sauce from the chicken into a small saucepan and sprinkle it with the cornflour. Stir the cornflour into the marinade, bring the mixture to the boil and simmer, stirring frequently, for 5 minutes, or until it is thickened, then keep it warm.

3 Lightly brush the chargrill with oil and preheat it to low–medium direct heat and cook the chicken on the chargrill for 6–7 minutes on each side, or until it is cooked through. Toast the burger buns for about 1 minute on each side, or until they are marked and golden.

4 Spread some mayonnaise on the inside surface of each bun, cover the base with mizuna and cucumber ribbons, and top with the chicken. Spread some of the thickened marinade on top of the chicken, top with the other half of the bun and serve immediately.

❋ Note: Japanese mayonnaise will be available in larger supermarkets and Asian speciality stores. If you can't find it, use regular whole-egg mayonnaise instead.

ROAST SIRLOIN WITH MUSTARD PEPPER CRUST, POTATOES AND GRAVY

ROAST SIRLOIN WITH MUSTARD PEPPER CRUST AND HASSELBACK POTATOES

90 g (1/3 cup) Dijon mustard

2 tablespoons light soy sauce

2 tablespoons plain (all-purpose) flour

60 ml (1/4 cup) olive oil

3 teaspoons chopped thyme leaves

4 garlic cloves, crushed

2.5 kg (5 lb 8 oz) piece of sirloin, trimmed
  but with the fat still on top

6 potatoes

2 tablespoons butter, melted

1 onion, roughly diced

1 large carrot, roughly diced

2 celery stalks, roughly chopped

250 ml (1 cup) red wine

500 ml (2 cups) beef stock

2 bay leaves

2 teaspoons cornflour

SUITABLE FOR A COVERED BARBECUE
COOKING TIME: 1 HOUR 25 MINUTES
SERVES 6–8

1 Mix the mustard, soy sauce, flour, 2 tablespoons of the olive oil, 2 teaspoons of thyme, two of the crushed garlic cloves and 1 tablespoon of cracked black pepper in a small bowl.

2 Coat the sirloin with the mustard mixture, put it on a wire rack over a tray and refrigerate it for 1 hour so the crust sets.

3 To make the hasselback potatoes, boil the potatoes in their skins for 10–12 minutes, or until they are just cooked. Once they are cool enough to handle, peel and cut them in half lengthways. Make small even slices across the top of the potato, cutting only two-thirds of the way down, brush each one liberally with butter and season them well with salt and pepper.

4 Heat the remaining olive oil in a large saucepan, add the onion, carrot, celery and remaining garlic, and cook them for 5 minutes. Pour in the red wine, cook for another 5 minutes, then add the beef stock, the bay leaves and the remaining thyme. Mix the cornflour with 1 tablespoon water until it is smooth and add it to the pan. Simmer the sauce over low heat for 20 minutes, or until it is slightly thickened, then strain and season to taste with salt and pepper.

5 Preheat a kettle or covered barbecue to medium indirect heat, put the sirloin in the middle of the barbecue and arrange the potatoes arround it. Replace the cover and cook for 45 minutes.

6 Remove the sirloin from the barbecue, and leave it to rest, covered, for 10 minutes before carving. Serve the steak with the hasselback potatoes, asparagus and red wine sauce.

GRILLED ASPARAGUS

500 g (1 lb 2 oz) asparagus
2 tablespoons olive oil

Trim the woody ends from the
asparagus, toss them with the olive oil
and season well with salt and pepper.
Cook the asparagus on a preheated
chargrill plate, covered, for 5 minutes,
or until it is cooked through.

PIRI PIRI PRAWNS

1 kg (2 lb 4 oz) large raw prawns (shrimp)
4 long red chillies, seeded
185 ml ($^3/_4$ cup) white wine vinegar
2 large garlic cloves, chopped
6–8 small red chillies, chopped
125 ml ($^1/_2$ cup) olive oil
150 g ($5^1/_2$ oz) mixed lettuce leaves

SUITABLE FOR A FLAT OR RIDGED
  GRILL PLATE
COOKING TIME: 15 MINUTES
SERVES 4

1 Remove the heads from the prawns and slice them down the back without cutting right through, leaving the tail intact. Open out each prawn and remove the dark vein, then store the prepared prawns in the refrigerator while you make the sauce.

2 To make the sauce, put the long chillies in a saucepan with the vinegar and simmer them over medium–high heat for 5 minutes, or until the chillies are soft. Let the mixture cool slightly, then put the chillies and 60 ml ($^1/_4$ cup) of the vinegar in a food processor. Add the garlic and chopped small chillies, and blend until the mixture is smooth. While the motor is running, gradually add the oil and remaining vinegar to the food processor.

3 Put the prawns in the marinade, making sure they are well coated, then cover them and refrigerate for 30 minutes.

4 Take the prawns out of the marinade, bring the marinade to the boil and let it simmer for 5 minutes, or until it is slightly thickened and reduced. Take the prawns and the marinade out to the barbecue, and leave the saucepan with the marinade in it on the edge of the barbecue to keep warm.

5 Lightly oil the chargrill plate and heat it to high direct heat. Cook the prawns, basting them with the marinade, for 2–3 minutes on each side, or until they are cooked through. Arrange the lettuce on four plates, top it with the prawns and serve immediately with the chilli sauce.

CHIPOLATAS WITH CHEESE AND JALAPENO QUESADILLAS

2 tablespoons olive oil

2 garlic cloves, crushed

2 x 400 g (14 oz) tins crushed tomatoes

1/2 teaspoon ground cumin

16 x 15 cm (6 inch) flour tortillas

320 g (11 1/2 oz) coarsely grated Cheddar
cheese

60 g (1/3 cup) pickled Jalapeño chillies,
drained and roughly chopped

20 spicy chipolatas

coriander (cilantro) sprigs

SUITABLE FOR ANY BARBECUE
COOKING TIME: 1 HOUR
SERVES 4

1 Heat the olive oil in a frying pan over medium heat and cook the garlic for 1–2 minutes or until it is just beginning to turn golden. Add the crushed tomatoes and cumin, and season well. Reduce the heat to low and cook the relish for 30–35 minutes or until it becomes thick and pulpy.

2 While the relish is cooking, get to work on the quesadillas. Sprinkle a tortilla with 40 g (1/3 cup) of the grated cheese, leaving a 1 cm (1/2 inch) border around the edge. Scatter 1 1/2 teaspoons of the Jalapeño chillies over the cheese and put another tortilla on top, pressing it down. Repeat the process with the remaining tortillas, cheese and Jalapeños until you have eight quesadillas.

3 Preheat the barbecue to low direct heat. Cook the chipolatas on the flat plate, turning them occasionally, for 10–12 minutes or until they are cooked through. When the chipolatas are nearly ready, start cooking the quesadillas on the chargrill for 1–2 minutes on each side, or until the cheese has melted. You may need to do this in batches, so make sure you keep them warm as you go.

4 Cut each quesadilla into quarters and serve them with the tomato relish and chipolatas, garnished with the coriander.

GRILLED HALOUMI SALAD

1½ tablespoons lemon juice

2 tablespoons finely chopped mint leaves

125 ml (½ cup) olive oil

2 garlic cloves

8 slices ciabatta bread

300 g (10½ oz) haloumi cheese, cut into
   5 mm (½ inch) slices

3 ripe tomatoes

150 g (5½ oz) rocket (arugula) leaves

2 tablespoons pine nuts, toasted

SUITABLE FOR A FLAT OR RIDGED
   GRILL PLATE
COOKING TIME: 15 MINUTES
SERVES 4

1 Whisk the lemon juice, mint, 60 ml (¼ cup) olive oil and 1 clove of crushed garlic together, and season with salt and pepper.

2 Brush both sides of each slice of bread with 1 tablespoon of olive oil and season well. Brush the haloumi with 1 tablespoon of olive oil, then cut the tomatoes into 1 cm (½ inch) rounds, brush each round with 1 tablespoon olive oil and season them with salt and pepper.

3 Preheat the barbecue to medium direct heat and chargrill the bread for 1 minute on each side, or until it is golden and marked, then rub each piece on both sides with the remaining clove of garlic. Wrap the toast in foil and keep it warm on the side of the barbecue. Chargrill the haloumi and tomato for 3–5 minutes on each side, or until they are browned, then drizzle them with 1 tablespoon of the mint and lemon dressing.

4 Put the rocket and pine nuts in a large bowl and add the remaining dressing. Toss the salad gently until it is coated with the dressing, and pile some onto a piece of the garlic toast. Arrange some of the grilled haloumi and tomato across the top and serve it warm.

MARGARITA CHICKEN WITH AVOCADO AND GRAPEFRUIT SALAD

4 chicken breasts, skin on, tenderloin and
  any excess fat removed
60 ml (1/4 cup) tequila
60 ml (1/4 cup) lime juice
2 small chillies, finely chopped
3 garlic cloves, crushed
15 g (1/4 cup) finely chopped coriander
  (cilantro) leaves
1 tablespoon olive oil
lime wedges

AVOCADO AND GRAPEFRUIT SALAD
2 ruby grapefruit
1 ripe avocado
200 g (7 oz) watercress leaves
1 French shallot, finely sliced
1 tablespoon sherry vinegar
60 ml (1/4 cup) olive oil

SUITABLE FOR ANY BARBECUE
COOKING TIME: 15 MINUTES
SERVES 4

1 Put the chicken, tequila, lime juice, chilli, garlic, coriander and olive oil in a non-metallic bowl and mix it all together so that the chicken is coated in the marinade. Cover the bowl and refrigerate for at least 2 hours, or overnight.

2 Peel and segment the grapefruit, working over a bowl to save any juice drips for the dressing. Cut the avocado into 2 cm (3/4 inch) wedges and put it in a bowl with the watercress, grapefruit and shallot. Put 1 tablespoon of the reserved grapefruit juice into a small, screw-top jar with the sherry vinegar, olive oil, salt and black pepper, and shake it up. Pour the dressing over the salad and toss it gently.

3 Preheat the chargrill to medium–high direct heat. Remove the chicken breasts from the marinade, season them with salt and pepper, and grill for 7–8 minutes on each side or until they are cooked through.

4 Slice the chicken breasts on the diagonal and serve with the salad and some lime wedges.

GARLIC AND MINT LAMB SKEWERS WITH ALMOND COUSCOUS AND YOGHURT SAUCE

8 lamb fillets, trimmed and cut into 2.5 cm
   (1 inch) cubes
2 tablespoons olive oil
80 ml (1/3 cup) lemon juice
2 garlic cloves, crushed
2 teaspoons dried mint leaves

YOGHURT SAUCE
250 g (1 cup) thick Greek-style yoghurt
1 garlic clove, crushed

ALMOND COUSCOUS
370 g (2 cups) instant couscous
1 tablespoon olive oil
500 ml (2 cups) chicken stock
40 g (1 1/2 oz) butter
2 teaspoons ras el hanout (see Note)
35 g (1/4 cup) currants, soaked in warm
   water for 10 minutes
60 g (1/2 cup) slivered almonds, toasted
25 g (1/2 cup) chopped mint leaves

SUITABLE FOR ANY BARBECUE
COOKING TIME: 10 MINUTES
SERVES 4

1 Put the lamb in a non-metallic bowl with the olive oil, lemon juice, garlic and mint. Stir the pieces around so that they are well coated and season with black pepper. Cover and refrigerate for at least 4 hours, or overnight.

2 Make the yoghurt sauce by mixing the yoghurt and garlic in a small bowl, then refrigerate it until you are ready to use it.

3 Put the couscous in a heatproof bowl, drizzle it with the olive oil and season well with salt. Bring the chicken stock to the boil and pour it over the couscous, then cover the bowl and leave it for 10 minutes to absorb the stock. Add the butter and fluff it through with a fork until it has melted and the grains are separated. Stir in the ras el hanout, currants, almonds and mint, and season to taste with salt and pepper.

4 Soak eight wooden skewers in cold water for 1 hour, then thread the lamb onto them and season well. Preheat the barbecue to medium–high direct heat and grill the skewers for 3–4 minutes on each side, or until they are cooked to your liking. Serve the skewers on a bed of couscous with the yoghurt sauce.

✻ Note: Ras el hanout is a fragrant spice blend used in Moroccan cooking and is available from specialist food stores. If you can't find it, you can make your own (see the recipe on page 65).

CHINESE-STYLE BARBECUE SPARERIBS

60 ml (¼ cup) hoisin sauce

80 ml (⅓ cup) oyster sauce

2 tablespoons rice wine

125 ml (½ cup) soy sauce

6 garlic cloves, crushed

3 teaspoons finely grated fresh ginger

2 kg (4 lb 8 oz) American-style pork ribs

2 tablespoons honey

SUITABLE FOR A COVERED BARBECUE
COOKING TIME: 50 MINUTES
SERVES 6

1 Mix the hoisin sauce, oyster sauce, rice wine, soy sauce, garlic and ginger in a large, non-metallic bowl, add the ribs and turn them so that they are coated in the marinade. Cover the bowl and refrigerate for at least 4 hours, or overnight.

2 Remove the ribs from the marinade and tip the marinade into a small saucepan with the honey. Simmer the mixture over low heat for 5 minutes, or until it becomes slightly syrupy — you will be using this to baste the ribs as they cook.

3 Heat a kettle or covered barbecue to medium indirect heat and cook the ribs, covered, for 10 minutes, then turn them over and cook them for another 5 minutes. Continue cooking, basting and turning the ribs frequently for 30 minutes, or until they are cooked through and caramelized all over.

4 Once the ribs are cooked, let them rest, covered, for 10 minutes. Cut the racks into individual ribs to serve and make sure there are plenty of napkins available — these ribs should be eaten with your fingers and are quite sticky.

BEEF FAJITAS

800 g (1 lb 12 oz) rump steak

2 teaspoons cumin

1 teaspoon ground oregano

1 teaspoon paprika

2 tablespoons Worcestershire sauce

1 tablespoon soy sauce

3 garlic cloves

60 ml (1/4 cup) lime juice

1 large onion, thinly sliced

1 red capsicum (pepper), cut into 5 mm
    (1/4 inch) strips

1 green capsicum (pepper), cut into 5 mm
    (1/4 inch) strips

1 tablespoon olive oil

8 flour tortillas

1 ripe avocado, diced

2 ripe Roma (plum) tomatoes, diced

60 g (1/2 cup) grated Cheddar cheese

90 g (1/3 cup) sour cream

SUITABLE FOR A FLAT OR RIDGED
    GRILL PLATE

COOKING TIME: 20 MINUTES

SERVES 4–6

1 Trim the steak of any fat and give it a good pounding with a meat mallet on both sides. Mix the cumin, oregano, paprika, Worcestershire sauce, soy sauce, garlic and lime juice in a shallow, non-metallic dish and add the beef. Turn the meat so that it is well coated in the marinade, then cover and refrigerate for at least 4 hours, or overnight.

2 Drain the steak, reserving the marinade, and pat it dry with paper towels. Put the marinade in a small saucepan, bring it to the boil and simmer it over medium heat for 5 minutes, or until it is reduced by about half, and keep it warm.

3 Preheat a barbecue to high direct heat. Toss the onion and capsicum with the oil then spread them across the flat plate, turning every so often for 10 minutes, or until they are cooked through and caramelized. While the vegetables are cooking, grill the steak on the chargrill plate for 3 minutes on each side, or until it is cooked to your liking, then remove it from the heat and let it rest, covered, for 5 minutes. Thinly slice the steak and arrange it on a plate with the onion and capsicum strips and serve them with the tortillas, avocado, tomato, cheese, sour cream and marinade sauce. Let everyone fill their own tortillas with some of each ingredient.

THAI RED CHICKEN WITH JASMINE RICE AND ASIAN GREENS

1 tablespoon red curry paste

250 g (1 cup) coconut cream

3 kaffir lime leaves

4 chicken breast fillets, skin on, tenderloin
   removed

400 g (2 cups) jasmine rice

250 ml (1 cup) chicken stock

1 tablespoon soy sauce

1 garlic clove, bruised

2 x 2 cm (3/4 x 3/4 inch) piece fresh ginger,
   bruised

750 g (1 lb 10 oz) Chinese broccoli, washed
   and tied in a bunch

coriander (cilantro) sprigs

SUITABLE FOR A FLAT OR RIDGED
   GRILL PLATE

COOKING TIME: 30 MINUTES

SERVES 4

1 Mix together the curry paste, coconut cream and kaffir lime leaves, then add the chicken and turn it so that it is coated in the marinade. Cover the bowl and refrigerate it for at least 4 hours, or overnight.

2 Half an hour before you are ready to cook the chicken, wash the rice in a sieve until the water runs clear. Put the rice in a saucepan with 750 ml (3 cups) water and bring it to the boil for 1 minute. Cover the saucepan with a tightly fitting lid, reduce the heat to as low as possible and let it cook for 10 minutes. Without removing the lid, remove the pan from the heat and leave it for at least 10 minutes, or until you are ready to eat. Meanwhile, bring the chicken stock, soy sauce, garlic and ginger to the boil in a small saucepan for 5 minutes, or until it is reduced by half. Strain the mixture, return the liquid to the saucepan and keep it warm.

3 Bring a large pot of salted water to the boil and add the Chinese broccoli, stalk side down. Cook for 2–3 minutes or until it is just tender, then drain well and arrange it on a serving dish. Just before serving, pour the hot chicken stock mixture over the greens.

4 Preheat the flat grill plate to medium direct heat. Cook the chicken, skin side down first, for 7–8 minutes on each side, or until it is cooked through. Transfer the chicken to a plate, cover it loosely with foil and leave it to rest. Fluff the rice with a fork and put it in a serving bowl. Garnish the chicken with coriander sprigs and serve it with the rice and greens.

ROAST RACK OF PORK WITH CHUNKY APPLE SAUCE AND VEGETABLES

6 Granny Smith apples

90 g (1/3 cup) sugar

60 ml (1/4 cup) white vinegar

2 tablespoons finely shredded mint leaves

1 rack of pork with 6 ribs (about 1.6 kg/
  3 lb 8 oz)

1 tablespoon olive oil

ROASTED VEGETABLES

2 orange sweet potatoes

1 kg (2 lb 4 oz) piece pumpkin

12 small onions

6 carrots

80 ml (1/3 cup) olive oil

6 garlic cloves, unpeeled

2 tablespoons finely chopped flat-leaf
  (Italian) parsley

SUITABLE FOR A COVERED BARBECUE
COOKING TIME: 1 HOUR 40 MINUTES
SERVES 6

1 Peel the apples, remove the seeds, and roughly dice the flesh. Simmer them over low heat with the sugar, vinegar and 60 ml (1/4 cup) water in a small saucepan for 15 minutes, or until they are cooked through and just beginning to collapse. Remove the sauce from the heat and stir in the shredded mint.

2 Score the skin on the rack of pork in a large diamond pattern, rub the oil all over the pork, then rub 1 teaspoon salt into the skin. To make the roast vegetables, peel the sweet potato, pumpkin, onions and carrots, and cut them into large, even pieces. Gently toss the vegetables with 2 tablespoons of olive oil until they are coated, and season them well with salt and freshly ground black pepper. Trim the root end from the garlic cloves, drizzle 1/2 teaspoon of oil over them and wrap them in a double layer of foil.

3 Preheat a kettle or covered barbecue to medium indirect heat. Put the pork rack in the middle of the barbecue, cover it and roast for 1 hour 20 minutes, or until the juices run clear when a skewer is inserted into the thickest part of the flesh. When the pork has been cooking for about 20 minutes, arrange the vegetables around the roast and cook them, covered, for 1 hour or until they are golden and tender. Add the garlic to the barbecue and cook it for 30 minutes or until it has softened.

4 When the garlic cloves are cool enough to handle, squeeze them from their skin, mash them with the remaining olive oil and stir in the chopped parsley. Season with salt and pepper, and drizzle the dressing over the roast vegetables just before serving.

5 When the pork is cooked, remove it from the barbecue, and leave it to rest, covered, for 10 minutes. Slice between the bones and serve it with the roasted vegetables and chunky apple sauce.

SPANISH-STYLE SEAFOOD SALAD WITH ROMESCO SAUCE

SPANISH-STYLE SEAFOOD SALAD

8 raw Balmain bugs (slipper lobsters)

1 kg (2 lb 4 oz) raw king prawns (jumbo shrimp)

500 g (1 lb 2 oz) baby squid tubes, cleaned

125 ml (1/2 cup) olive oil

3 garlic cloves, finely chopped

15 g (1/4 cup) chopped basil leaves

80 ml (1/3 cup) lemon juice

150 g (5 1/2 oz) rocket (arugula) leaves

150 g (5 1/2 oz) frisée lettuce

2 tablespoons extra virgin olive oil

1 tablespoon red wine vinegar

SUITABLE FOR A FLAT OR RIDGED
  GRILL PLATE
COOKING TIME: 15 MINUTES
SERVES 4

1 To prepare the bugs, cut into the membrane where the head and body join, then twist off the tail and discard the head. Use kitchen scissors to cut down both sides of the underside shell, working the scissors between the flesh and shell, then peel back the undershell and throw it away. To prepare the prawns, remove the heads and legs, leaving the shells and tails intact. Turn each prawn on its back and cut a slit through the centre of each prawn lengthways, taking care not to cut all the way through. Open out the prawn to form a butterfly and remove the dark vein from the back, starting at the head end. Wash the squid and pat them dry with paper towels, then cut a small slit in the base of the tubes so that they open up when cooking.

2 Mix together the oil, garlic, basil and lemon juice in a large bowl, add the seafood and toss so that it is coated in the marinade. Cover the bowl and refrigerate it for 30 minutes.

3 Just before you cook the seafood, toss the salad leaves with the olive oil and vinegar, and refrigerate, covered, until you are ready to eat.

4 Heat the barbecue chargrill plate to very high direct heat. Cook the bugs for 5–6 minutes, or until the shells turn pink and the flesh starts pulling away from the shells. Halfway through cooking the bugs, add the prawns and cook them, flesh side down, for 2–3 minutes. Turn and cook for another 2–3 minutes, or until they are pink and cooked through. Add the squid after turning the prawns, and cook them for 1–2 minutes, or until they are brown, marked and just cooked through. Remove all of the seafood from the barbecue as soon as it is just done, as residual heat will continue to cook the meat. Arrange the salad leaves on a serving plate, top them with the barbecued seafood and drizzle with the Romesco sauce. Serve the salad immediately, with any remaining Romesco sauce on the side and crusty bread rolls to soak up all of the juices.

ROMESCO SAUCE

80 ml (⅓ cup) olive oil

¼ teaspoon paprika

1 small red capsicum (pepper),
  seeded and quartered lengthways

3 ripe Roma (plum) tomatoes

2 long red chillies

50 g (⅓ cup) blanched almonds and
  hazelnuts, toasted

3 garlic cloves, crushed

1 tablespoon red wine vinegar

1 tablespoon lemon juice

Preheat the barbecue to medium direct heat. Mix half of the olive oil with the paprika, add the capsicum, tomatoes and chillies, and toss. Cook the capsicum and tomatoes on the chargrill plate for 5 minutes, then add the chillies and cook for another 5 minutes or until the tomatoes are softened and the vegetables are charred. Peel the capsicum and tomatoes when they are cool, then remove the seeds and skin from the chilli. Process the nuts until they are finely ground. Add the vegetables, garlic, vinegar and juice, and blend to a paste. Slowly add the remaining oil and season to taste. If the sauce is too thick, add 2 tablespoons of water to get it to a pouring consistency.

143

STUFFED EGGPLANT

2 eggplants (aubergines)

2 tablespoons olive oil

1 onion, chopped

2 garlic cloves, crushed

4 tomatoes, roughly chopped

2 teaspoons tomato paste (tomato purée)

2 tablespoons chopped dill leaves

2 tablespoons chopped flat-leaf (Italian)
   parsley leaves

2 tablespoons currants

2 tablespoons pine nuts

1 tablespoon red wine vinegar

150 g (1 1/2 cups) finely grated kefalotyri
   cheese

SUITABLE FOR A COVERED BARBECUE

COOKING TIME: 45 MINUTES

SERVES 4

1 Cut each eggplant in half lengthways and use a sharp knife to cut out the flesh, leaving a 5 mm (1/4 inch) thick shell. Finely dice the flesh, toss it with 2 teaspoons of salt and drain it in a colander over a bowl for 30 minutes. Squeeze out any excess moisture from the eggplant, rinse it under cold water and drain well on paper towels.

2 Heat 1 tablespoon oil in a frying pan over high heat. Add the diced eggplant and cook it, stirring frequently, for 5 minutes, or until it is browned, then put it in a large bowl. Heat the remaining olive oil in the frying pan over medium heat, cook the onion and garlic for 2 minutes, then add the tomato, tomato paste, dill, parsley, currants, pine nuts and vinegar. Stir it all together and cook it for 8–10 minutes, stirring occasionally. Add the tomato mixture to the eggplant with 50 g (1 cup) of the kefalotyri, season with black pepper and mix it together well.

3 Spoon the vegetable mixture into the eggplant shells and sprinkle the remaining cheese over the top. Preheat a kettle or covered barbecue to medium indirect heat and put the stuffed eggplants in the middle of the barbecue, cover them and cook for 30 minutes, or until they are cooked through. This vegetarian treat is delicious with a green salad.

HONEY MUSTARD CHICKEN WITH SPRING ONION MASH

175 g (½ cup) honey

60 g (¼ cup) Dijon mustard

2 tablespoons oil

2 tablespoons white wine vinegar

3 garlic cloves, crushed

2 tablespoons chopped parsley leaves

1 x 1.8 kg (4 lb) chicken, cut into 10 serving
   pieces

SPRING ONION MASH

1 kg (2 lb 4 oz) floury (starchy) potatoes

2 tablespoons butter

80 ml (⅓ cup) milk

60 ml (¼ cup) cream

3 spring onions (scallions), finely sliced

SUITABLE FOR A COVERED BARBECUE
COOKING TIME: 45 MINUTES
SERVES 4–6

1 Put the honey, mustard, oil, white wine vinegar, garlic, parsley and ¼ teaspoon freshly ground black pepper in a large, non-metallic bowl. Mix it all together well, and put aside 60 ml (¼ cup) of the marinade to baste the chicken during cooking. Add the chicken pieces to the rest of the marinade and turn them so that they are thoroughly coated. Cover the bowl and refrigerate it for at least 4 hours, or overnight.

2 To make the spring onion mash, peel the potatoes and cut them into large chunks. Steam or boil the pieces for 12 minutes, or until they are tender, then drain the water away and briefly return the potato to the heat, shaking the pan, to dry any excess moisture. Add the butter, milk and cream, and mash the potato until it is smooth and lump-free. Stir in the spring onion, season to taste and keep the potato warm while you cook the chicken.

3 Preheat a covered or kettle barbecue to medium indirect heat and cook the chicken pieces for 20–30 minutes, or until they are cooked through. The breast pieces may take as little as 15 minutes, while dark meat will take longer. Baste the chicken with the reserved marinade during the last 5–8 minutes of cooking, but no earlier or it is likely to burn. Serve the chicken on a bed of spring onion mash.

CRISPY-SKINNED SALMON SALAD NIÇOISE

400 g (14 oz) kipfler potatoes, washed

1 tablespoon olive oil

sea salt

12 quail eggs

300 g (10½ oz) small green beans

2 teaspoons olive oil, extra

3 x 200 g (7 oz) salmon fillets

2 large ripe tomatoes, cut into 8 wedges

150 g (5½ oz) small black olives

80 ml (⅓ cup) extra virgin olive oil

1½ tablespoons white wine vinegar

1 tablespoon lemon juice

2 garlic cloves, crushed

SUITABLE FOR A FLAT OR RIDGED
   GRILL PLATE
COOKING TIME: 20 MINUTES
SERVES 4

1 Boil or steam the potatoes for 10 minutes or until they are almost cooked through. Drain and cut them into 2 cm (¾ inch) slices on the diagonal, then toss them with the olive oil until they are coated and season to taste with sea salt.

2 Put the eggs in a saucepan of cold water and bring them to the boil for 2 minutes. Cool the eggs under running water, then peel and halve them. Bring the water back to the boil and cook the beans for 2 minutes or until they are just tender, then drain them, plunge them into cold water and drain again.

3 Heat the barbecue to medium–high direct heat. Cook the potato slices on the chargrill plate for 2 minutes on each side, or until they are golden and cooked through. Brush the salmon fillets with the extra oil and cook them, skin side down, on the flat plate for 2–3 minutes, then turn and cook them for another 2–3 minutes, or until they are almost cooked through. The salmon should remain slightly rare in the middle. Break the fillets into chunks with a fork, removing any bones as you go.

4 Put the potato in a large bowl with the beans, tomato and olives. Whisk together the oil, vinegar, lemon juice and garlic, and add the dressing to the bowl. Season with sea salt and freshly ground black pepper, and gently toss the salad until everything is well combined. Pile some of the potato mixture on four serving plates, top with the salmon and eggs, and serve immediately.

CHILLI BEEF BURGER WITH PINEAPPLE MINT SALSA

BURGERS

500 g (1 lb 2 oz) minced (ground) beef

6 Asian shallots, finely chopped

25 g (¼ cup) crisp fried onion flakes
  (see Note)

3 garlic cloves, finely chopped

2 long red chillies, seeded and finely
  chopped

20 g (⅓ cup) finely chopped coriander
  (cilantro) leaves (include some stems)

2–2½ tablespoons chilli garlic sauce
  (see Note)

1 egg, lightly beaten

160 g (2 cups) fresh breadcrumbs

PINEAPPLE MINT SALSA

1 small ripe pineapple

1 tablespoon grated palm sugar or soft
  brown sugar

1 small red chilli, seeded and finely diced

½ teaspoon rice vinegar

2 tablespoons lime juice

4 spring onions (scallions), finely chopped

15 g (¼ cup) chopped mint leaves

olive oil, for brushing

1 loaf Turkish bread, cut into 4 pieces, or
  4 round Turkish rolls

100 g (3 handfuls) mignonette or green oak
  lettuce leaves

SUITABLE FOR ANY BARBECUE

COOKING TIME: 15 MINUTES

SERVES 4

1 To make the burgers, put the mince, shallots, onion flakes, garlic, chilli, coriander, chilli garlic sauce, egg, breadcrumbs and 1½ teaspoons of salt in a large bowl, and knead it well with your hands, working all of the ingredients through until they are thoroughly combined. Cover the bowl and refrigerate it for 2 hours.

2 Meanwhile, to make the pineapple salsa, peel the pineapple, remove all of the eyes and slice it lengthways into quarters. Remove the central core and cut the flesh into 1 cm (½ inch) dice. Put the pineapple in a non-metallic mixing bowl with the remaining salsa ingredients and stir them together, then cover the bowl and refrigerate for 1 hour to let the flavours develop.

3 Using wet hands, divide the mince mixture into four equal portions, roll each portion into a ball, then flatten it slightly to form patties. When you are ready to cook the burgers, preheat the chargrill plate to medium direct heat. Brush the patties lightly with oil and grill them for 5–6 minutes, then flip them and cook for another 5–6 minutes, or until they are well browned and cooked through. A few minutes before the patties are done, toast the bread, cut side down, on the chargrill plate for 1–2 minutes, or until it is marked and golden.

4 To assemble the burgers, divide the lettuce among four of the toasted bread slices. Add a pattie and top with some of the pineapple and mint salsa. Season the burgers with salt and pepper, then top with the remaining toasted bread and serve them straight away.

 Note: Crisp fried onion flakes and chilli garlic sauce are available from Asian grocery stores.

ROSEMARY LAMB ON GRILLED POLENTA WITH ANCHOVY SAUCE

600 g (1 lb 5 oz) lamb fillets

1 tablespoon finely chopped rosemary
   leaves

3 garlic cloves, bruised

2 tablespoons olive oil

1 tablespoon lemon juice

250 g (1²/₃ cups) instant polenta

35 g (¹/₃ cup) grated Parmesan cheese

20 g (¹/₂ oz) butter

60 g (1¹/₂ cups) rocket (arugula) leaves

ANCHOVY AND ROSEMARY SAUCE

8 large anchovy fillets, chopped

3 teaspoons finely chopped rosemary leaves

150 ml (7 tablespoons) olive oil

1 tablespoon lemon juice

SUITABLE FOR ANY BARBECUE
COOKING TIME: 30 MINUTES
SERVES 4

1 Trim the lamb fillets of any fat and sinew, and put them in a non-metallic bowl with the rosemary, garlic, olive oil and lemon juice, turning the fillets until they are well coated. Season with pepper, cover the bowl and refrigerate it for at least 4 hours, or overnight.

2 Meanwhile, to make the polenta, bring 1 litre of salted water to the boil in a heavy-based saucepan. Whisking constantly, add the polenta in a thin stream and stir until it thickens and starts to come away from the side of the pan. Remove the pan from the heat and add the Parmesan and butter, then season generously with salt and freshly ground black pepper. Stir the polenta until the cheese and butter have melted, then pour it into a lightly greased 22 cm (9 inch) square baking tin and smooth the surface. Refrigerate the polenta for 2 hours or until it is cool and firm, then turn it out onto a chopping board, trim the edges and cut the block into four squares.

3 While the polenta is cooling, make the anchovy and rosemary sauce. Put the anchovies and rosemary in a food processor and blend them to a paste. Add the olive oil in a thin stream, then add the lemon juice and season to taste.

4 Preheat the chargrill plate to medium direct heat. Grill the polenta squares for 7–8 minutes on each side or until they are crisp and golden. When the polenta is ready, move the squares to the side of the grill, season the lamb fillets with salt and cook them for 2–3 minutes on each side for medium–rare, or until they are cooked to your liking.

5 To serve, slice the lamb fillets into four pieces on the diagonal, cutting across the grain. Put the grilled polenta on warmed serving plates, top it with the lamb and rocket and drizzle with the sauce.

FIVE-SPICE ROAST CHICKEN

1.8 kg (4 lb) chicken

1 tablespoon soy sauce

2 garlic cloves, crushed

1 teaspoon finely grated fresh ginger

1 tablespoon honey

1 tablespoon rice wine

1 teaspoon five-spice

1 tablespoon peanut oil

SUITABLE FOR A COVERED BARBECUE
COOKING TIME: 1 HOUR 10 MINUTES
SERVES 4

1 Wash the chicken and pat it thoroughly dry inside and out with paper towels. Whisk the soy sauce, garlic, ginger, honey, rice wine and five-spice together in a small bowl and brush it all over the chicken, ensuring every bit of skin is well coated. Put the chicken on a wire rack over a baking tray and refrigerate it, uncovered, for at least 8 hours, or overnight.

2 Preheat a kettle or covered barbecue to medium indirect heat and put a drip tray under the rack. Brush the chicken liberally with the peanut oil and put it breast side up in the middle of the barbecue over the drip tray. Cover the barbecue and roast the chicken for 1 hour 10 minutes, or until the juices run clear when you pierce it with a skewer between the thigh and body. Check the chicken every so often, and if it appears to be over-browning, cover it loosely with foil. Leave it to rest, covered, for 10 minutes before carving and serving. The flavours in this style of chicken go particularly well with steamed Asian greens and fried rice.

LOBSTER WITH BURNT BUTTER SAUCE AND GRILLED LEMON

150 g (5½ oz) butter

60 ml (¼ cup) lemon juice

2 tablespoons chopped flat-leaf (Italian)
  parsley leaves

1 small garlic clove, crushed

8 lobster tails in the shell

2 lemons, cut into wedges

SUITABLE FOR ANY BARBECUE
COOKING TIME: 15 MINUTES
SERVES 8

1 Melt the butter in a small saucepan over medium heat and cook it for 3 minutes or until it begins to brown, but watch it carefully to make sure that it doesn't burn. Lower the heat, and cook the butter for another 2 minutes, or until it is a dark, golden brown. Remove the pan from the heat, add the lemon juice, parsley and garlic, and season with salt and freshly ground black pepper.

2 Cut the lobster tails lengthways and remove any digestive tract, but leave the meat in the shell. Preheat the chargrill plate to medium direct heat and brush the exposed lobster meat with lots of the butter mixture. Cook the lobster tails, cut side down, on the chargrill plate for 6 minutes, then turn them over and cook for another 3–5 minutes, or until the shells turn bright red. While the lobster is cooking, put the lemon wedges on the hottest part of the chargrill and cook them for 1 minute on each side, or until they are marked and heated through. Arrange the lobster on a serving plate and serve it with the grilled lemon wedges and the rest of the warm brown butter as a dipping sauce. This is delicious with a green salad and some crusty bread to soak up the juices.

CHILLI BEAN TORTILLA WRAPS WITH GUACAMOLE AND SALSA

CHILLI BEAN TORTILLA WRAPS

CHILLI BEANS

2 tablespoons olive oil

2 garlic cloves, crushed

1 onion, finely chopped

1 green capsicum (pepper), seeded, cored
   and chopped

2 small red chillies, seeded and finely
   chopped

1/2 teaspoon cayenne pepper

1 teaspoon paprika

1 teaspoon ground cumin

1/4 teaspoon sugar

440 g (15 1/2 oz) tin crushed tomatoes

440 g (15 1/2 oz) tin red kidney beans,
   drained and rinsed

1 tablespoon tomato paste (tomato purée)

12 x 20 cm (8 inch) soft flour tortillas

225 g (8 oz) Cheddar cheese, coarsely
   grated

250 g (1 cup) sour cream

coriander (cilantro) sprigs to garnish

1 lime, cut into 8 wedges

SUITABLE FOR ANY BARBECUE

COOKING TIME: 50 MINUTES

SERVES 4

1 To make the chilli beans, heat the oil in a saucepan over low heat and cook the garlic, onion and capsicum, stirring frequently, for 8–10 minutes, or until the onion and capsicum have softened. Add the chilli, cayenne pepper, paprika, cumin, sugar, tomato, beans, tomato paste and 125 ml (1/2 cup) water. Bring the mixture to the boil, then reduce the heat and let it simmer for 15–20 minutes, or until it is thickened and reduced. Season to taste.

2 To assemble the wraps, put some of the chilli beans along the middle of each tortilla, sprinkle it with 2 tablespoons of the cheese and roll it up. Put three rolls, seam side down, on a double layer of foil and seal the foil to form a parcel. Preheat the flat plate to low–medium direct heat and grill the parcels for 6–8 minutes on each side or until they are heated through.

3 Unwrap the foil parcels and slide the tortillas onto serving plates. Top them with the guacamole, sour cream and salsa, garnish with coriander sprigs and serve them with the lime wedges.

GUACAMOLE

2 ripe avocados, mashed

2½ tablespoons lime juice

3 spring onions (scallions), finely sliced

15 g (¼ cup) chopped coriander
  (cilantro) leaves

1 teaspoon finely chopped red chilli

Combine the avocado, lime juice,
spring onion, coriander and chilli, and
season the mixture to taste. Cover the
guacamole with plastic wrap, resting
the plastic directly on the surface of
the mixture, and refrigerate until you
are ready to use it.

SALSA

4 ripe tomatoes, finely diced

40 g (¼ cup) finely chopped red onion

25 g (½ cup) chopped coriander
  (cilantro) leaves

1 tablespoon lime juice

Combine the tomato, onion, coriander
and lime juice, season to taste, then
cover the salsa with plastic wrap and
refrigerate. Remove the salsa from the
refrigerator 15 minutes before you are
ready to use it so the ingredients have
time to return to room temperature and
their full flavour.

161

PORK SKEWERS IN GREEN GINGER WINE AND SOY MARINADE WITH CHARGRILLED SPRING ONION BULBS

800 g (1 lb 12 oz) pork fillets, trimmed

1 tablespoon finely grated fresh ginger

2 garlic cloves, finely chopped

1 tablespoon finely chopped preserved
   ginger in syrup

60 ml (1/4 cup) green ginger wine (see Note)

2 1/2 tablespoons kecap manis

1/2 teaspoon sesame oil

1 tablespoon oil

8 bulb spring onions, green parts removed,
   quartered

1 tablespoon olive oil

coriander (cilantro) sprigs

SUITABLE FOR A FLAT OR RIDGED
   GRILL PLATE

COOKING TIME: 10 MINUTES

SERVES 4

1 Cut the pork fillets into 12 cm x 2.5 cm (5 inch x 1 inch) strips and put them in a non-metallic bowl with the ginger, garlic, preserved ginger, green ginger wine, kecap manis and oils, turning the meat to make sure it is evenly coated. Cover and refrigerate the bowl, and leave it to marinate for at least 2 hours, or overnight. Soak twelve wooden skewers in cold water for 1 hour, then thread four pork strips into an S-shape onto each skewer. Cover the skewers and refrigerate them until you are ready to start cooking.

2 Preheat the barbecue to medium direct heat. Toss the spring onions with the olive oil and season them with salt and freshly ground black pepper. Cook them on the flat plate for 10 minutes, or until they are softened and well browned. When the spring onions are nearly cooked, put the kebabs on the chargrill plate and grill them for 2 minutes on each side, or until the pork is just cooked through and glazed. Garnish the skewers with coriander sprigs and serve them immediately with the spring onion.

✳ Note: Green ginger wine is a sweet, fortified wine with a distinctive ginger flavour which originated in Britain. The best known brands are Stone's and Crabbie's.

TUNA STEAKS WITH SALSA AND GARLIC MASH

GARLIC MASH

1 kg (2 lb 4 oz) floury (starchy) potatoes,
   cut into chunks
6–8 garlic cloves, peeled
80 ml (⅓ cup) milk
60 ml (¼ cup) olive oil

SALSA

1 tablespoon olive oil
2 French shallots, finely chopped
200 g (7 oz) green olives, pitted and
   quartered lengthways
35 g (¼ cup) currants, soaked in warm
   water for 10 minutes
1 tablespoon baby capers, rinsed and
   squeezed dry
1 tablespoon sherry vinegar
2 tablespoons shredded mint leaves

4 tuna steaks (about 150 g/5½ oz each)
olive oil, for brushing
sea salt

SUITABLE FOR ANY BARBECUE
COOKING TIME: 20 MINUTES
SERVES 4

1 Boil the potato and garlic for 10–15 minutes, or until they are tender. Drain them, then return the pan to the heat, shaking it to evaporate any excess water. Remove the pan from the heat and mash the potato and garlic until they are smooth, then stir in the milk and olive oil, and season with salt and freshly ground black pepper.

2 To make the salsa, heat the oil in a frying pan over medium heat. Add the shallots and cook them for 2–4 minutes, or until they are softened, but not browned, then add the olives, drained currants and capers. Cook everything for 2 minutes, stirring it continuously, add the vinegar and cook for another 2 minutes, or until the liquid is reduced by about half. Remove the pan from the heat and keep the salsa warm until you're ready to dish up.

3 Preheat the chargrill plate to medium–high direct heat. Brush the tuna steaks with olive oil, season them well with sea salt and freshly ground black pepper, and grill for 2–3 minutes on each side for medium–rare, or until they are cooked to your liking. Stir the mint into the salsa and serve it immediately with the garlic mash and tuna.

SPICY BUFFALO WINGS WITH RANCH DRESSING

12 large chicken wings

2 teaspoons garlic salt

2 teaspoons onion powder

oil, for deep-frying

125 ml (1/2 cup) tomato sauce

2 tablespoons Worcestershire sauce

50 g (1 3/4 oz) butter, melted

Tabasco sauce, to taste

RANCH DRESSING

1 small garlic clove, crushed

185 g (3/4 cup) mayonnaise

125 ml (1/2 cup) buttermilk

2 tablespoons finely chopped flat-leaf
    (Italian) parsley

1 tablespoon finely chopped chives

1 1/2 teaspoons lemon juice

1 1/2 teaspoons Dijon mustard

1 teaspoon onion powder

SUITABLE FOR A FLAT OR RIDGED
    GRILL PLATE

COOKING TIME: 30 MINUTES

SERVES 4

1 Pat the wings dry with paper towels, remove and discard the tip of each wing, then cut them in half at the joint to create two pieces. Combine the garlic salt, onion powder and 2 teaspoons of ground black pepper, and rub the spice mixture into each chicken piece.

2 Deep-fry the chicken in batches for 2–3 minutes without letting it brown, then remove the pieces from the oil and drain them on crumpled paper towels. Once the chicken has cooled down a little, put it in a non-metallic bowl with the combined tomato sauce, Worcestershire sauce, butter and Tabasco, and toss so that all of the pieces are well coated in the marinade. Cover and refrigerate the bowl for at least 2 hours, or overnight.

3 To make the ranch dressing, mash the garlic and 1/4 teaspoon salt to a paste then add the mayonnaise, buttermilk, parsley, chives, lemon juice, mustard and onion powder, and whisk it all together. Season well, cover and refrigerate for at least 1 hour before serving.

4 Preheat the barbecue to medium direct heat. Cook the chicken for 6–8 minutes on each side, or until it is caramelized and sticky, turning and basting with the marinade as it cooks. Serve the chicken hot with the ranch dressing.

It's time to round off the meal and tempt everyone with a mouthwatering dessert. Why go back into the kitchen? Make good use of the residual heat in your barbecue as it cools down to the perfect temperature after your main course. Clean off the grill and get mouths watering again with the scent of warm fruits and syrups wafting through the air. Just sit back and enjoy the compliments — there's no need to admit how easy it was!

desserts

GRILLED PANETTONE WITH PEACHES

125 g (1/2 cup) caster (superfine) sugar
1/2 vanilla bean, halved and scraped
1 tablespoon Grand Marnier
4 ripe peaches
oil, for brushing
4 large slices panettone
80 g (1/3 cup) crème fraîche

SUITABLE FOR ANY BARBECUE
COOKING TIME: 15 MINUTES
SERVES 4

1 Put the sugar, vanilla bean and 60 ml (1/4 cup) water in a small saucepan and stir over low heat until the sugar has dissolved. Simmer the mixture, without stirring it, for 10 minutes, then remove it from the heat, stir in the Grand Marnier and keep it warm.

2 Dip the peaches into a saucepan of boiling water for 5 seconds then refresh them under cold water and remove the skins, which should slip off easily. Cut the peaches in half, remove the stone and lightly brush the cut side with oil. Preheat the chargrill plate to medium direct heat and grill the peaches, cut side down, for 5 minutes, or until they are golden and warmed through. Grill the panettone for 30 seconds to 1 minute on each side, or until it is marked and lightly toasted. The panettone will brown very quickly, so be careful to not burn it. Arrange the grilled peaches over the panettone, drizzle with the vanilla syrup and serve with a scoop of crème fraîche.

BERRY AND MARSHMALLOW GRATIN

600 g (1 lb 5 oz) mixed seasonal berries
   (strawberries, raspberries, blueberries,
   blackberries) (see Note)
2 tablespoons raspberry liqueur
150 g (5^1/$_2$ oz) pink and white marshmallows
vanilla ice cream

SUITABLE FOR A COVERED BARBECUE
COOKING TIME: 10 MINUTES
SERVES 6

1 Put the berries and raspberry liqueur in a bowl, stir them gently to coat the berries and transfer them to a 1.5 litre ceramic ovenproof dish. Top the berries with the marshmallows, making sure they are evenly distributed over the surface.

2 Preheat a covered or kettle barbecue to medium–high indirect heat and put the dish in the middle of the barbecue. Let it cook for 8–10 minutes or until the berries are bubbling and the marshmallow has puffed up and is starting to melt. Serve the gratin immediately with a big scoop of ice cream, but take care to not burn your mouth on the berries, which will be very hot.

✳ Note: If it's not berry season, and your berries are not as sweet as they should be, add a little caster (superfine) sugar with the liqueur. Use strawberries in a smaller proportion to the other berries as they tend to release a lot of liquid.

FRUIT SKEWERS WITH RUM BUTTER GLAZE

1 peach, peeled, stoned and cut into
  8 pieces
1 mango, peeled, stoned and cut into
  8 pieces
8 strawberries, hulled and halved
160 g (5½ oz) papaya, cut into 8 pieces
160 g (5½ oz) pineapple, cut into 8 pieces
2 bananas, cut into 2 cm (¾ inch) pieces
185 ml (¾ cup) dark rum
80 g (⅓ cup) dark brown sugar
1 tablespoon butter
ice cream

SUITABLE FOR A FLAT OR RIDGED
  GRILL PLATE
COOKING TIME: 20 MINUTES
SERVES 4

1 Put the peach, mango, strawberries, papaya, pineapple and banana in a bowl with the rum and sugar, and stir gently until all of the fruit is coated in the marinade. Cover and refrigerate the bowl for 1 hour.

2 Soak eight wooden skewers in cold water for 1 hour. Drain the marinade into a small, heavy-based saucepan and thread the fruit onto the skewers. Make sure each skewer has a good mix of fruits and that the pieces are not crowded, or they won't cook evenly.

3 Bring the marinade to the boil over medium heat, then reduce the heat and simmer it for 5 minutes, or until it is reduced and syrupy. Remove the pan from the heat and whisk in the butter until it becomes smooth and glossy.

4 Preheat the flat grill plate to medium direct heat and cook the skewers for 5–8 minutes on each side, or until they are golden, basting them all over with the rum glaze during the last minute of cooking. Arrange the skewers on a serving plate, drizzle them with the rum glaze and serve warm with ice cream.

COCONUT PANCAKES WITH GRILLED BANANAS AND SYRUP

150 g (5½ oz) palm sugar, roughly
   chopped, or soft brown sugar
2 tablespoons lime juice
125 g (1 cup) plain (all-purpose) flour
45 g (¼ cup) rice flour
125 g (½ cup) caster (superfine) sugar
45 g (½ cup) desiccated coconut
500 ml (2 cups) coconut milk
2 eggs, lightly beaten
4 bananas, sliced thickly on the diagonal
2 tablespoons dark brown sugar
50 g (1¾ oz) butter, plus 20 g (1 oz) extra
30 g (½ cup) shredded coconut, toasted
1 lime, cut into wedges

SUITABLE FOR A FLAT GRILL PLATE
COOKING TIME: 45 MINUTES
SERVES 4

1 Put the palm sugar in a small, heavy-based saucepan with 125 ml (½ cup) water and stir it over low heat for 5 minutes, or until the sugar has dissolved. Increase the heat to medium and let it simmer, without stirring, for 15 minutes, or until the liquid becomes a thick, sticky syrup. Stir in the lime juice and keep the syrup warm.

2 Sift the plain and rice flour together, add the caster sugar and desiccated coconut, and stir it all together. Make a well in the middle and pour in the combined coconut milk and egg, beating until the mixture is smooth.

3 Preheat the flat plate to low–medium direct heat. Toss the bananas in the dark brown sugar and grill them around the cooler edges of the flat plate, dotting each piece with butter. Cook the banana, turning the pieces occasionally, for 4–5 minutes, or until it begins to soften and brown. Melt a little of the extra butter in the middle of the plate and pour on 60 ml (¼ cup) of the pancake mixture, using the back of a spoon to spread it out to a 15 cm (6 inch) circle. Cook the pancake for 2–3 minutes, or until the underside is golden, then turn it over and cook the other side for another minute. As each pancake is cooked, transfer it to a plate and cover it with a tea towel to keep it warm. Add more butter to the hot plate as necessary and keep going until all of the pancake mix has been used.

4 Fold each pancake into quarters and put two on each serving plate. Top them with grilled banana, drizzle each with a little palm sugar syrup, sprinkle with the coconut and serve with lime wedges.

CAMEMBERT WITH PORT-SOAKED RAISINS

2 tablespoons raisins
2 tablespoons port
365 g (12 oz) whole Camembert cheese
oil spray
almond bread

SUITABLE FOR A FLAT OR RIDGED
  GRILL PLATE
COOKING TIME: 10 MINUTES
SERVES 4

1 Put the raisins and port in a small saucepan over high heat until they just come to the boil, then allow the mixture to cool for about 30 minutes.

2 Cut a circular lid from the top of the Camembert, leaving a 2 cm (3/4 inch) border. Carefully remove the lid, and scoop out the soft cheese with a teaspoon, leaving the base intact. Put the raisins in the hole and top with the cheese, squashing it down so that as much as possible fits back into the cavity, then replace the lid.

3 Spray a double layer of foil with canola spray and wrap the Camembert to form a sealed parcel. Preheat the flat plate to low direct heat and cook the parcel for 8–10 minutes, or until it is heated through and soft. Make sure the heat stays low, or the rind will go brown and burn. Serve with the almond bread.

✳ Note: After cooking your main feast, there should be just enough heat left in the barbecue to warm the Camembert for this delicious dessert.

AMARETTI-STUFFED APPLES WITH VANILLA RICOTTA

2 tablespoons sultanas

2 tablespoons amaretto

10 small amaretti biscuits (about 60 g/
  2¼ oz)

2 tablespoons slivered almonds, toasted

1 tablespoon sugar

2½ tablespoons butter, melted

4 Granny Smith apples

VANILLA RICOTTA

½ vanilla bean

2 tablespoons icing (confectioners') sugar

250 g (1 cup) ricotta cheese

SUITABLE FOR A COVERED BARBECUE
COOKING TIME: 20 MINUTES
SERVES 4

1 Soak the sultanas in the amaretto for 15 minutes or until they are softened, then add them to the crushed amaretti with the amaretto, almonds, sugar and 2 tablespoons of melted butter.

2 Scrape the seeds out of the vanilla bean and add them and the icing sugar to the ricotta. Use an electric beater to beat the mixture until the ricotta is smooth and creamy.

3 Remove the apple cores and enough fruit from around the core to make a hole about 2.5 cm (1 inch) across. Stuff the hole with the amaretto mixture, brush the apples with the remaining melted butter and wrap them securely in foil. Preheat a kettle or covered barbecue to low–medium indirect heat, put the apples on the barbecue and cook them, covered, for 15–20 minutes, or until they are tender. Serve with a big scoop of the vanilla ricotta.

✳ Note: Vanilla ricotta is a delicious alternative to whipped or double cream to serve with desserts.

PINEAPPLE WITH BROWN SUGAR GLAZE AND TOASTED COCONUT

1 pineapple
115 g (1/2 cup) dark brown sugar
1/2 teaspoon vanilla essence
1 tablespoon Galliano
60 g (1/4 cup) butter
2 tablespoons coconut flakes, toasted
vanilla ice cream

SUITABLE FOR ANY BARBECUE
COOKING TIME: 25 MINUTES
SERVES 6

1 Peel the pineapple and remove all the eyes, then slice it lengthways into quarters and remove the core. Cut the fruit into long 1 cm (1/2 inch) wide wedges.

2 Put the brown sugar, vanilla essence and 2 teaspoons water in a small saucepan and cook it over low–medium heat for 5 minutes, or until the sugar has dissolved. Remove the pan from the heat, add the Galliano, then return the pan to the heat and simmer the mixture for 3 minutes. Whisk in the butter and continue to simmer the mixture over low heat for 15 minutes, or until it is smooth and thick.

3 Preheat the chargrill plate to medium direct heat, brush the pineapple pieces with the brown sugar glaze, and grill them for 2–3 minutes, or until grill marks appear. Arrange the pineapple pieces on a serving platter, top them with the glaze and the toasted coconut, and serve with vanilla ice cream.

PEAR AND HAZELNUT CREPES WITH CINNAMON SUGAR

CREPES

250 g (2 cups) plain (all-purpose) flour
3 eggs
375 ml (1 1/2 cups) milk
60 g (1/4 cup) butter, melted
melted butter, extra, for cooking

FILLING

500 g (2 cups) cream cheese
2 tablespoons icing (confectioners') sugar,
   sifted
80 g (2/3 cup) hazelnuts, toasted, skinned
   and roughly chopped
150 g (2/3 cup) candied peel
2 teaspoons finely grated lemon zest
2 tablespoons Frangelico or Poire William
1 large firm green pear, cored and cut into
   1 cm (1/2 inch) dice

2 tablespoons caster (superfine) sugar
1 teaspoon ground cinnamon

SUITABLE FOR ANY BARBECUE
COOKING TIME: 25 MINUTES
MAKES 12 CREPES

1 To make the crêpe batter, sift the flour into a bowl with a pinch of salt and make a well. Gradually whisk in the combined eggs and milk until the batter is smooth, then stir in the melted butter. Strain the batter into a jug, cover and refrigerate it for 1 hour. The consistency should be similar to thin cream, so add a little more milk if it looks too thick.

2 To make the filling, beat the cream cheese and icing sugar in a bowl until smooth. Add the hazelnuts, peel, zest and liqueur, and stir it all together. Gently stir in the diced pear and refrigerate the filling until you are ready to use it.

3 Heat an 18 cm (7 inch) crêpe or non-stick frying pan over low–medium heat and brush it with butter. Pour 60 ml (1/4 cup) of batter into the pan, and swirl it around so that the bottom of the pan is thinly covered. Cook the crêpe for 1 minute or until the edges just begin to curl, then turn it over and cook the other side for 30 seconds. Slide the crêpe out of the pan onto a plate and continue with the remaining batter, stacking the crêpes as they cook.

4 Put 2 heaped tablespoons of the filling in the middle of each crêpe, fold two opposite sides in to the middle and flatten the mixture slightly, then fold in the other two sides to enclose the filling.

5 Preheat the flat plate to low direct heat and cook the crêpe parcels for 3–4 minutes on each side, or until they are golden and crisp, and the filling is warmed through. Transfer the parcels to serving plates, sprinkle them with the combined caster sugar and cinnamon, and serve them immediately.

✳ Note: If you are making the crêpes in advance, stack them between sheets of greaseproof paper to stop them from sticking to each other. Do not refrigerate.

GLOSSARY

BASTE   to spoon or brush cooking juices or other fat over food during cooking to prevent it from drying out, or to help with heat transfer.

BROWN   to pan-fry, bake, grill or roast food (often meat) so the outer surface turns a golden brown colour.

CARAMELIZE   to cook until sugars, which either exist naturally in the food or are added (for example in a marinade), become golden brown.

CHARGRILL   a heavy metal plate with slotted grill bars which allows the food to be directly exposed to the heat and fire below for a true barbecue flavour. It may also refer to this method of cooking food.

CHARRED   food cooked on a chargrill until the surface is blackened.

CORE   to remove the core from fruit by using either a corer or a small sharp knife.

COVERED BARBECUE   refers to a barbecue that has a fitted lid which may be closed to make it suitable for roasting or slow cooking.

DICE   to chop food into very small, even cubes. Use a very sharp knife to do this.

DRIP TRAY   used in kettle barbecues for indirect cooking. It is placed between the fuel briquettes to catch any dripping juices.

DRY-FRY   to cook spices in a dry frying pan until they become fragrant. Keep a close eye on spices cooked in this way, as they can burn in a very short space of time.

FILLET   to cut the meat, fish or poultry away from the bone. It also refers to the particular cut of meat (e.g. pork or lamb), commonly taken from the top half of an animal's leg.

FLAT GRILL PLATE   a heavy, flat metal plate set over a heat source which doesn't allow the flames from the barbecue to actually touch the food. This means that there are no flare-ups caused by dripping juices or fat.

GLAZE   to coat food with a liquid as it is cooking. A glaze adds flavour, colour and shine.

GREASE   to lightly coat a tin or dish with oil or melted butter to prevent food from sticking.

HEAVY-BASED SAUCEPAN   usually has a copper lining in the base which allows for even and constant distribution of heat across the whole base of the pan.

KETTLE BARBECUE   refers to a rounded barbecue with a lid.

MARINATE   to tenderize and flavour food (usually meat) by leaving it in an acidulated seasoned liquid (a marinade).

NON-METALLIC DISH   a ceramic or glass dish which will not react with any acids in the foods stored or marinated in it.

PARBOIL   to partially cook a food in boiling water before some other form of cooking. Most commonly used for roast potatoes, which are parboiled before being added to the roasting tin.

PUREE   food blended or processed to a pulp.

REDUCE   to boil or simmer liquid in an uncovered pan so that the liquid evaporates and the mixture becomes thicker and more concentrated in flavour.

REST   to allow meat to sit, covered, for a period of time after it has cooked before slicing it. This enables the muscle fibres to relax and so retain the juices when cut.

RUB   a mixture of dried herbs and spices used as a dry marinade for foods, usually meat.

SCORE   to make incisions with a knife (usually into fish or meat) in a crossed pattern, without cutting all the way through. This ensures even cooking through thicker sections of the food.

SEGMENT   to use a small sharp knife to cut sections of citrus fruit away from the pith and membrane.

SHRED   to cut food into small, narrow strips, either by hand, or using a grater or food processor with a shredding disc. Cooked meat may be shredded by pulling it apart with forks or your fingers.

SIMMER   to cook liquid, or food in a liquid, over low heat, just below boiling point. The surface of the liquid should be moving, with a few small bubbles coming to the surface.

SKIM   to remove fat or scum that comes to the surface of a liquid.

SMOKE   adding fragrant woodchips to the barbecue heat source to produce smoke which will impart a distinctive flavour to the food as it cooks. Works best with barbecue briquettes.

STRAIN   to remove solids from a liquid by pouring it through a sieve. The solids are discarded, unless otherwise specified.

SYRUP   a sweetened liquid which has been reduced by simmering to a thicker consistency.

ZEST   the coloured skin of citrus fruits, usually lemon, orange and lime. It is often grated and added to mixtures, but avoid the bitter white pith.

COOKING TIMES GUIDE

The cooking temperature in a kettle or covered barbecue is not always constant, so we've provided these times to use as a guide. Take the time to get to know your barbecue and you will become more confident with this style of cooking.

beef

BEEF per 500 g	WITH A BONE	BONELESS
rare	15 minutes	10 minutes
medium	20 minutes	15 minutes
well done	25 minutes	20 minutes

lamb

LEG OF LAMB per 500 g	
medium rare	10–15 minutes
medium	20–25 minutes
well done	30 minutes

pork

PORK
allow 30 minutes per 500 g
Pork should be cooked through, but not overcooked or the flesh will be dry. Test that it is ready by inserting a skewer into the thickest part of the pork, or close to the bone; the juices should be clear with no trace of pink.

poultry

POULTRY
allow 20–25 minutes per 500 g
It's important that chicken is cooked right through with no pink flesh or juices inside. Check by inserting a skewer between the thigh and the body through to the bone; the juices should run clear.

fish

FISH
allow 20–25 minutes per 500 g
Different varieties of fish require different cooking times. Tuna and salmon steaks are often cooked medium rare, as the flesh tends to become dry if cooked through. Depending on thickness, they may only need a few minutes on each side over direct heat. Most other fish are served cooked through. It is important that they are removed from the barbecue as soon as they are ready, as residual heat in the flesh will continue to cook the meat. Test by inserting a thin-bladed knife into the thickest part of the fish; it will be ready when the flesh flakes cleanly.

INDEX

This edition published in 2003 by Whitecap Books Ltd.
For more information, contact Whitecap Books, 351 Lynn Avenue,
North Vancouver, British Columbia, V7J 2C4

Editorial Director: Diana Hill

Editor: Katharine Gasparini

Creative Director: Marylouise Brammer

Concept design: Michelle Cutler

Design: Michelle Cutler, Alex Frampton

Calligraphy: Genevieve Huard

Food Directors: Lulu Grimes, Jane Lawson

Food Editor: Vanessa Broadfoot

Recipe Writers: Vanessa Broadfoot, Ross Dobson, Kathleen Gandy,
Jane Lawson, Christine Osmond, Rebecca Truda

Cooks: Vanessa Broadfoot, Ross Dobson, Kathleen Gandy,
Christine Osmond, Rebecca Truda

Photographer: Alan Benson

Stylist: Jane Hann

Food: Vanessa Broadfoot

Chief Executive: Juliet Rogers

Publisher: Kay Scarlett

Production Manager: Kylie Kirkwood

Printed by Toppan Printing Hong Kong Co. Ltd. PRINTED IN CHINA.

ISBN 1-55285-482-5

We have used 20 ml tablespoon measures. If you are using a 15 ml tablespoon, for most recipes the difference will not be noticeable. However, for recipes using small amounts of flour and cornflour, add an extra teaspoon for each tablespoon specified. We have used 60 g (Grade 3) eggs in all recipes.

IMPORTANT: Those who might be at risk from the effects of salmonella poisoning (the elderly, pregnant women, young children and those suffering from immune deficiency diseases) should consult their GP with any concerns about eating raw eggs.

The Publisher would like to thank the following for their assistance with photography: AEG Kitchen Appliances, Liebherr Refrigeration and Wine Cellars; Bertolli Olive Oil; Breville Holdings Pty Ltd; Chief Australia; Kitchen Aid; Sheldon & Hammond, with special thanks to Woodland Home Products Pty Ltd and Weber Australia for providing the barbecues.